THE 1982 TAX/BENEFIT POSITION
OF A TYPICAL WORKER
IN OECD MEMBER COUNTRIES

LA SITUATION
D'UN OUVRIER MOYEN EN 1982
AU REGARD DE L'IMPÔT
ET DES TRANSFERTS SOCIAUX
DANS LES PAYS MEMBRES DE L'OCDE

ORGANISATION FOR ECONOMIC CO-OPERATION AND DEVELOPMENT
ORGANISATION DE COOPÉRATION ET DE DÉVELOPPEMENT ÉCONOMIQUES

Pursuant to article 1 of the Convention signed in Paris on 14th December, 1960, and which came into force on 30th September, 1961, the Organisation for Economic Co-operation and Development (OECD) shall promote policies designed:

- to achieve the highest sustainable economic growth and employment and a rising standard of living in Member countries, while maintaining financial stability, and thus to contribute to the development of the world economy;
- to contribute to sound economic expansion in Member as well as non-member countries in the process of economic development; and
- to contribute to the expansion of world trade on a multilateral, non-discriminatory basis in accordance with international obligations.

The Signatories of the Convention on the OECD are Austria, Belgium, Canada, Denmark, France, the Federal Republic of Germany, Greece, Iceland, Ireland, Italy, Luxembourg, the Netherlands, Norway, Portugal, Spain, Sweden, Switzerland, Turkey, the United Kingdom and the United States. The following countries acceded subsequently to this Convention (the dates are those on which the instruments of accession were deposited): Japan (28th April, 1964), Finland (28th January, 1969), Australia (7th June, 1971) and New Zealand (29th May, 1973).

The Socialist Federal Republic of Yugoslavia takes part in certain work of the OECD (agreement of 28th October, 1961).

Also available

REVENUE STATISTICS OF OECD MEMBER COUNTRIES 1965-1982 (July 1983)
(23 83 04 3)   ISBN 92-64-024530   210 pages, bilingual   £9.20   US$18.00   F92.00

INCOME TAX COLLECTION LAGS (July 1983)
(23 83 03 1) ISBN 92-64-12466-7   54 pages   £4.00   US$8.00   F40.00

INCOME TAX SCHEDULES: DISTRIBUTION OF TAXPAYERS AND REVENUES (December 1981)
(23 81 03 1)   ISBN 92-64-12257-5   44 pages   £2.90   US$6.50   F29.00

THE IMPACT OF CONSUMPTION TAXES AT DIFFERENT INCOME LEVELS (June 1981)
(21 81 02 1)   ISBN 92-64-12212-5   66 pages   £3.20   US$8.00   F32.00

THE TAX BENEFIT POSITION OF SELECTED INCOME GROUPS IN OECD MEMBER COUNTRIES 1974-1979 (January 1981)
(23 80 02 1)   ISBN 92-64-12132-3   212 pages, bilingual   £7.60   US$19.00   F76.00

THE TAXATION OF NET WEALTH, CAPITAL TRANSFERS AND CAPITAL GAINS OF INDIVIDUALS (March 1979)
(23 79 01 1)   ISBN 92-64-11896-9   196 pages   £10.80   US$22.00   F88.00

Prices charged at the OECD Publications Office.

*THE OECD CATALOGUE OF PUBLICATIONS and supplements will be sent free of charge
on request addressed either to OECD Publications Office,
2, rue André-Pascal, 75775 PARIS CEDEX 16, or to the OECD Sales Agent in your country.*

Également disponible

STATISTIQUES DE RECETTES PUBLIQUES DES PAYS MEMBRES DE L'OCDE 1965-1982 (juillet 1983)
(23 83 04 3)   ISBN 92-64-02453-0   210 pages, bilingue   F92.00   £9.20   US$18.00

DÉLAIS DE RECOUVREMENT DES IMPÔTS SUR LE REVENU (juillet 1983)
(23 83 03 2) ISBN 92-64-22466-1   62 pages   F40.00   £4.00   US$8.00

BARÈME DE L'IMPÔT SUR LE REVENU. RÉPARTITION DES CONTRIBUABLES ET DES RECETTES (décembre 1981)
(23 81 03 2)   ISBN 92-64-22257-X   44 pages   F29.00   £2.90   US$6.50

L'INCIDENCE DES IMPÔTS SUR LA CONSOMMATION A DIFFÉRENTS NIVEAUX DE REVENUS (juin 1981)
(21 81 02 2)   ISBN 92-64-22212-X   68 pages   F32.00   £3.20   US$8.00

LA SITUATION AU REGARD DE L'IMPÔT ET DES TRANSFERTS SOCIAUX DE CERTAINS GROUPES DE REVENU DANS LES PAYS MEMBRES DE L'OCDE 1974-1979 (janvier 1981)
(23 80 02 2)   ISBN 92-64-22132-8   212 pages, bilingue   F76.00   £7.60   US$19.00

L'IMPOSITION DES PERSONNES PHYSIQUES SUR LA FORTUNE, LES MUTATIONS, ET LES GAINS EN CAPITAL (mars 1979)
(23 79 01 2)   ISBN 92-64-21896-3   216 pages   F88.00   £10.80   US$22.00

Prix de vente au public dans la librairie du Siège de l'OCDE.

*LE CATALOGUE DES PUBLICATIONS et ses suppléments seront envoyés gratuitement
sur demande adressée soit au Bureau de Vente des Publications de l'OCDE,
2, rue André-Pascal, 75775 PARIS CEDEX 16, soit au dépositaire des publications
de l'OCDE de votre pays.*

TABLE OF CONTENTS

TABLE DES MATIERES

FOREWORD

    This report represents the latest in a regular series by the Committee on Fiscal Affairs on the impact of payments of personal income taxes and employees' social security contributions and receipts of universal cash transfers for dependent children on the disposable income of typical family units at the level of average earnings in the manufacturing sector for male production workers. Its aim is to provide the most recent comparable quantitative data on the position of taxpayers in OECD countries and to show how these positions have changed during the last few years.

AVANT-PROPOS

Le présent rapport est le dernier en date d'une série que le Comité des Affaires Fiscales consacre périodiquement à l'étude de l'incidence sur le revenu disponible d'une unité familiale type d'un ouvrier moyen de sexe masculin dans l'industrie manufacturière, des versements qu'elle effectue au titre de l'impôt sur le revenu des personnes physiques et des cotisations salariales de sécurité sociale, ainsi qu'aux effets des prestations en espèces perçues par toutes les familles ayant des enfants à charge. Il a pour objet de présenter les données quantitatives comparables les plus récentes sur la position des contribuables dans les pays de l'OCDE et d'indiquer comment celle-ci s'est modifiée au cours des dernières années.

I. SCOPE AND LIMITATIONS

A. UNIT OF COMPARISON

1.   This report looks at the tax/benefit position of taxpayers at the
income level of a typical production worker. In selecting the unit of
comparison, the choice was to a large extent determined by the need for
comparable data from all Member countries. This rules out a percentile
income approach as, although many countries possess data on income distribution, they are calculated in different ways. Comparable data, however,
are available for average earnings of full-time male manual workers in the
manufacturing industry. Details of these data are given in paragraphs 9
to 11. Comparisons of the tax payable on such earnings (usually referred
to as the earnings of the average production worker, APW) in Member countries have been made over a number of years(1). Data are available on the
tax payable and benefits received by single people and married couples
with two children.

B. TAXES AND BENEFITS COVERED

2.   The report is concerned with personal income tax and employees' social security contributions payable in respect of earnings and family
benefits received in the form of universal cash transfers. Income tax on
unearned income and indirect taxes are not considered, although employers'
social security contributions are referred to. Both central and local
government income taxes are included in the data, although no detailed
description is provided of local taxes(2). Tax reliefs taken into account
include the basic allowances, the allowance for marriage, and allowances
for children, but allowances for specific expenditures and other allowances which are not received by all taxpayers in the circumstances specified in the report are excluded. The family benefits taken into account
are those received by families with two children at the specified age
levels.

---

1. The most recent publication of the results of these comparisons
is, "The tax/benefit position of selected income groups, 1974-1978", OECD,
Paris, October 1980.
2. However, in France, the "taxe d'habitation", a local tax on the
use of immovable property, although resembling a local income tax, is excluded from the study because of the diversity of the rates applied. This
exclusion does not significantly affect the results of the study.

I. PORTEE ET LIMITES DE L'ETUDE

A. UNITES COMPAREES

1.   Le présent rapport étudie la situation à l'égard de l'impôt et des avantages sociaux des contribuables au niveau du revenu d'un ouvrier moyen. Le choix de l'unité de comparaison a été, dans une large mesure, déterminé par la nécessité de disposer de données comparables fournies par tous les pays Membres. Ce qui explique qu'on ait dû renoncer à la méthode des percentiles ; en effet, si de nombreux pays possèdent des statistiques sur la répartition des revenus, celles-ci sont établies suivant des méthodes différentes. Toutefois, on possède des statistiques comparables sur le salaire moyen des travailleurs manuels de sexe masculin employés à temps complet dans l'industrie manufacturière. On trouvera des renseignements détaillés sur ces statistiques aux paragraphes 9 à 11. Les impôts dus sur ce salaire (dit en général salaire de l'ouvrier moyen, OM) dans les pays Membres ont été comparés sur un certain nombre d'années (1). Des données sont disponibles concernant l'impôt dû et les prestations perçues par les célibataires, et par les couples mariés ayant deux enfants.

B. IMPOTS ET PRESTATIONS CONSIDERES

2.   Le rapport considère l'impôt sur le revenu des personnes physiques et les cotisations salariales de sécurité sociale dus sur les salaires, ainsi que les prestations familiales perçues sous forme de transferts en espèces. Il laisse de côté l'impôt sur les revenus qui ne dérivent pas du travail et les impôts indirects, mais fait toutefois brièvement allusion aux cotisations patronales de sécurité sociale. Les impôts sur le revenu sont ceux qui sont perçus par l'administration centrale et par les administrations locales bien que pour ces dernières on n'ait pas procédé à une description détaillée des impôts perçus (2). Les allégements fiscaux dont on a tenu compte comprennent les abattements de base, l'abattement en raison du mariage et les abattements pour enfants à charge, mais on a exclu les abattements correspondant à des dépenses particulières et les autres abattements dont tous les contribuables ne bénéficient pas dans les cas prévus par le rapport. Les prestations familiales considérées sont celles que perçoivent

---

1. La publication la plus récente concernant les résultats de ces comparaisons est la brochure intitulée "La situation d'un ouvrier moyen au regard de l'impôt et des transferts sociaux, 1974-1978", OCDE, Paris, octobre 1980.
2. Toutefois, pour la France, la taxe d'habitation, impôt local sur l'usage de biens immobiliers, bien qu'elle soit assimilable à un impôt local sur le revenu, est exclue du champ de l'étude en raison de la diversité des taux pratiqués. Cette exclusion n'a pas d'incidence sensible sur les résultats de l'étude.

C. PERIOD COVERED

3.   The report refers to the year 1982, although the comparative tables and charts cover the period 1978 to 1982. Detailed information for earlier years can be found in the publication "The tax/benefit position of selected income groups, 1972-1976", OECD, 1978.

D. LIMITATIONS

4.   The simple approach of comparing the tax/benefit position of the APW avoids many of the conceptual and definitional problems involved in more complex approaches but it must be realised that whilst the APW himself is working in the manufacturing sector in each country and is therefore pro- bably doing similar kinds of work, an APW's earnings will probably occupy a different position in the distribution of earnings in each country, de- pending upon the dispersion of earnings.

5.   Because of the limitations on the taxes and benefits covered in the report, the data cannot be taken as an indication of the overall impact of the government sector on the welfare of taxpayers and their families. Complete coverage would require not only studies of the impact of indirect taxes, the treatment of unearned income under personal income taxes and the effect of other tax allowances and cash benefits, but also considera- tion of the effect on welfare of services provided by the State either free or below cost and the incidence of corporate and other direct taxes on earnings and household prices. Such a broad coverage is difficult, if not impossible, in a single country, let alone for the purpose of an international comparison. The differences between the results shown here and those that would be shown by a full study of the overall impact of government would no doubt vary from one country to another depending, mainly, on the relative shares of different kinds of taxes in government revenues(3) and on the scope and nature of government social expenditures.

6.   The income left at the disposal of a taxpayer may represent different standards of living in different countries because the range of goods and services on which the income is spent and their relative prices differ as between countries. In those countries where a wide range of public goods and services is provided (free health services, public housing, etc.) the taxpayer may be left with less cash income but may enjoy the same living standards as a taxpayer receiving a higher cash income but living in a country where there are less State-provided goods and services.

7.   The limitations on the tax reliefs covered and the exclusion of other types of income mean that the effective rates of income tax calculated in this report will not necessarily reflect the actual rates paid by tax- payers at the level of earnings shown. On the one hand, the actual rates may be lower than the calculated effective rates because the latter do not take into account non-standard reliefs; on the other hand, the actual rates may be higher than the calculated rates because the latter do not take into account tax on sources of income other than earnings.

---

3. The relative shares of the taxes included in this study as a per- centage of both total taxation and GDP are shown in "Revenue Statistics of OECD Member countries 1965 to 1982", Paris 1983.

les familles ayant à charge des enfants qui font partie des tranches d'âge précisées.

C. PERIODES CONSIDEREES

3.   Le rapport couvre l'année 1982 bien que les tableaux comparatifs et les graphiques se refèrent aux années 1978 à 1982. Pour les années précédentes, on peut trouver des renseignements comparables dans la publication intitulée "La situation au regard de l'impôt et des transferts sociaux de certains groupes de revenus 1972-1976", OCDE, 1978.

D. LIMITES

4.   En utilisant la méthode simple qui consiste à comparer la situation au regard de l'impôt et des avantages sociaux de l'ouvrier moyen, on échappe aux nombreux problèmes de théorie et de définition que soulèvent des méthodes plus complexes ; mais il faut bien se rendre compte que si l'ouvrier moyen lui-même est un travailleur qui, dans chaque pays, exerce son activité dans l'industrie manufacturière et accomplit donc des tâches du même type, sa situation dans l'éventail des salaires varie selon la disperson de ceux-ci dans chaque pays.

5.   Les limites inhérentes aux impôts et aux transferts sociaux considérés dans le présent rapport, font que les données réunies ne peuvent être considérées comme représentatives de l'incidence générale du secteur public sur le niveau de vie des contribuables et de leur famille. Il faudrait pour cela, non seulement étudier l'incidence des impôts indirects et le régime auquel les impôts sur le revenu des personnes physiques soumettent les revenus autres que ceux du travail, mais aussi l'incidence des autres abattements fiscaux et des prestations en espèces, sans oublier d'envisager l'incidence sur le niveau de vie des services fournis par l'Etat, soit gratuitement, soit en-dessous de leur coût, et aussi l'incidence des impôts sur les sociétés et d'autres impôts directs sur les salaires et sur les prix payés par les ménages. Il est difficile, voire impossible, de couvrir pour un seul pays, un champ d'études aussi étendu, sans parler de la difficulté des comparaisons sur le plan international. Les différences entre les résultats indiqués ici et ceux auxquels aboutirait une étude complète de l'incidence générale du secteur public, varieraient certainement d'un pays à l'autre, en fonction surtout de la part relative des différents impôts dans les recettes de l'Etat (3), et aussi de l'étendue et de la nature des dépenses à caractère social des entreprises publiques.

6.   Le revenu restant à la disposition du contribuable peut représenter des niveaux de vie différents selon les pays, parce que l'éventail des biens et services qu'on peut se procurer avec ce revenu et leur prix relatif, diffèrent selon les pays. Dans ceux où l'Etat fournit toute une série de biens et de services (services de santé gratuits, logements publics, etc.), le contribuable peut disposer finalement d'un revenu en espèce moindre, tout en bénéficiant du même niveau de vie qu'un contribuable percevant un revenu en espèces plus élevé, mais qui vit dans un pays où l'Etat fournit moins de biens et de services.

-----

3. Voir Statistiques de recettes publiques des pays de l'OCDE, 1965-1982, Paris, 1983.

8.   The report shows the formal incidence of personal income tax and employees' social security contributions on families and single people.
Nothing is said about who finally bears the burden of these taxes as this
depends upon how they are shifted and this is something upon which there
is still no agreement amongst economists. The results, however, do show
the proportion of gross earnings retained and this net cash income can be
seen as the amount over which the household is able to exercise a free
choice in the allocation of its expenditures. The data are comparable for
the specific situations set out in the definitions used and should not be
generalised to apply to other situations where different considerations
may apply.

E. DATA ON THE EARNINGS OF THE AVERAGE PRODUCTION WORKER

9.   The agreed definitions of the income and other characteristics of the
APW are given below with an indication of the countries for which comparable data could not be supplied:

    a) Sex of average worker male, except Canada, Italy, Portugal, Sweden
       and the United States which include both male and female workers.
    b) Normal overtime and other bonuses included.
    c) Unemployment benefit excluded.
    d) Sickness benefit paid by employer excluded except Australia.
    e) Age of children five to twelve years old.
    f) Calendar year except in Australia, Japan, New Zealand and the
       United Kingdom, where fiscal year figures are used.

10.   Different countries have had to build up gross earnings figures from
different bases hourly, daily, weekly or monthly. In all countries except
Australia this base has been used to produce an annual earnings figure by
taking the average of the weekly, monthly, etc., figures over the year.
In Australia, the necessary data are collected only in respect of one pay
period each year (in October) and the annual figure is derived by multi-
plying this average weekly earnings figure by 52. The sources of the
gross earnings data are given in Part IV.

11.   The earnings data do not necessarily relate to the same taxpayer
throughout the period. In each year, workers are identified on the basis
of the average earnings in manufacturing industry. As such, the results
do not refer to the changing earnings and tax/benefit position of particular individuals over time but rather to the position of workers earning
a wage equal to average earnings in manufacturing industry in each particular year.

7. Etant donné le nombre limité des allégements considérés et l'exclusion des autres catégories de revenus, les taux effectifs d'imposition qui sont indiqués peuvent ne pas rendre compte avec exactitude des taux effectivement payés par tous les contribuables se situant dans la tranche de revenu salarial considérée. D'un côté, l'exclusion des abattements autres que ceux de portée générale tend à surestimer les taux réels ; d'un autre côté, l'exclusion des revenus autres que ceux du travail (où des barèmes de taux plus élevés sont parfois appliqués) peut tendre à les sous-estimer.

8. Le rapport montre l'incidence formelle de l'impôt sur le revenu des personnes physiques et les cotisations salariales de sécurité sociale pour des familles. Il ne précise nullement qui supporte en définitive le fardeau de ces impôts, car cela est fonction des modalités de leur répercussion et c'est un point sur lequel les économistes ne sont pas encore tombés d'accord. Néanmoins, les résultats indiquent bien la proportion du salaire brut que conservent les familles que l'on a choisi d'étudier, et ce revenu net en espèces peut être considéré comme étant le montant grâce auquel une famille décide librement de la répartition de ses dépenses. Les données sont comparables pour les situations particulières qui sont précisées dans les définitions utilisées, mais il convient de ne pas les généraliser pour les appliquer à d'autres situations dans lesquelles des considérations différentes peuvent jouer.

E. DONNEES SUR LE SALAIRE DE L'OUVRIER MOYEN

9. On trouvera ci-après les définitions, généralement admises, du revenu et des autres caractéristiques de l'ouvrier moyen avec l'indication des pays pour lesquels des données comparables n'ont pu être fournies :

   a) Sexe de l'ouvrier moyen - masculin, sauf au Canada, aux Etats-Unis, en Italie, au Portugal et en Suède (masculin et féminin).
   b) Heures supplémentaires normales et autres primes - incluses.
   c) Indemnités de chômage - exclues.
   d) Indemnités de maladie à la charge de l'employeur - exclues, sauf en Australie.
   e) Age des enfants - 5 à 12 ans.
   f) Année civile sauf en Australie, au Japon, en Nouvelle-Zélande et au Royaume-Uni où l'on a utilisé l'année fiscale.

10. Certains pays ont dû calculer le salaire brut à partir de bases différentes : horaire, journalière, hebdomadaire ou mensuelle. Dans tous les pays, sauf en Australie, cette base a été utilisée pour le calcul du salaire annuel en prenant la moyenne annuelle des chiffres hebdomadaires, mensuels, etc. En Australie, les données nécessaires sont réunies pour une seule période de paie chaque année (en octobre) et le chiffre annuel est obtenu en multipliant ce gain moyen hebdomadaire par 52. On trouvera, dans la partie IV, l'indication des sources des statistiques sur le salaire brut.

11. Les données relatives aux salaires ne se réfèrent pas nécessairement aux mêmes contribuables pendant la période considérée. Pour chaque année, les ouvriers sont identifiés d'après le salaire moyen dans l'industrie manufacturière et d'après divers multiples de ce salaire. De ce fait, les résultats ne se réfèrent pas à l'évolution dans le temps de la situation de certains individus au regard de l'impôt et des transferts sociaux, mais plutôt à la situation d'ouvriers qui, pour une année déterminée, gagnent un salaire égal au salaire moyen dans l'industrie manufacturière.

II. COMPARATIVE TABLES AND CHARTS/TABLEAUX COMPARATIFS ET GRAPHIQUES

GENERAL FOOTNOTES

1. Data for 1982 are not available for Spain and Turkey.

2. Income taxes refer to central and local income taxes.

3. n.a. = not available.

4. The figures for New Zealand for 1978 to 1982 are not strictly comparable because the latter series refer to male workers only, whereas the former refer to all workers.

5. These tables do not take into account the exceptional surcharge on income tax applied in France in 1976 (applicable to 1975 income) as this can be paid in the form of a reimbursable loan to the State.

6. In Australia, "The Survey of Earnings and Hours" for 1981 was based upon a slightly wider sample than that used for previous years. However, this should not affect to any marked extent the comparability with previous years.

NOTES GENERALES

1. Les données pour 1982 ne sont pas disponibles pour l'Espagne et la Turquie.

2. Les impôts sur le revenu comprennent les impôts prélevés aux niveaux central et local.

3. n.d. = non disponible.

4. Les chiffres de la Nouvelle-Zélande pour 1978 à 1982 ne sont pas strictement comparables, car ces derniers se réfèrent à des ouvriers de sexe masculin, alors que les premiers se réfèrent à l'ensemble des ouvriers.

5. Ces tableaux ne tiennent pas compte de la majoration exceptionnelle appliquée en France en 1976 aux revenus de 1975 puisque dans tous les cas de schéma retenus ici, elle a pu être acquittée sous forme d'emprunt remboursable.

6. En Australie, "The Survey of Earnings and Hours" pour 1981 est basé sur un échantillon légèrement plus grand que celui utilisé pour les années précédentes. Cependant ceci ne devrait pas affecter la comparabilité avec les années précédentes.

Table/Tableau 1

INDICES OF GROSS EARNINGS, AFTER-TAX PAY, TAKE-HOME PAY, AND CONSUMER PRICES

INDICES DE SALAIRE BRUT, DE SALAIRE APRES IMPOT, DE REMUNERATION NETTE, ET DE PRIX A LA CONSOMMATION

Single people at the APW's income level

Célibataire avec un salaire égal de celui de l'OM

1982

1978 = 100

Country / Pays		Gross Earnings / Salaire brut	After-tax pay* / Salaire après impôt	Take-home pay** / Rémunération nette***	Consumer prices / Prix à la consommation
Australia – Australie	1980	124	123	123	120
	1981	143	140	140	133
	1982	157	155	155	148
Austria – Autriche	1980	116	116	116	110
	1981	124	123	122	118
	1982	131	131	129	124
Belgium – Belgique	1980	115	112	112	112
	1981	126	120	119	120
	1982	129	121	119	130
Canada – Canada	1980	120	119	119	120
	1981	134	133	132	135
	1982	149	146	146	150
Denmark – Danemark	1980	124	117	116	123
	1981	133	125	124	138
	1982	149	140	138	152
Finland – Finlande	1980	125	124	124	120
	1981	141	140	140	134
	1982	155	154	154	147
France – France (2)	1980	n.a.	n.a.	n.a.	n.a.
	1981	n.a.	n.a.	n.a.	n.a.
	1982	n.a.	n.a.	n.a.	n.a.
Germany – Allemagne	1980	114	114	113	110
	1981	119	119	118	116
	1982	122	123	121	122
Greece – Grèce (1)	1980	179	178	171	167
	1981	222	217	209	208
	1982	279	271	251	252
Ireland – Irlande	1980	132	131	131	134
	1981	155	153	152	161
	1982	172	170	164	189
Italy – Italie	1980	149	144	144	139
	1981	182	174	174	166
	1982	193	184	181	194
	1980	114	113	113	113

Country	Year				
	1982	131	130	130	131
Netherlands – Pays-Bas	1980	114	114	115	111
	1981	117	118	116	118
	1982	124	126	119	125
New Zealand – Nouvelle-Zélande	1980	137	138	138	135
	1981	150	151	151	155
	1982	177	175	175	179
Norway – Norvège	1980	112	110	108	116
	1981	123	125	123	132
	1982	136	138	135	147
Portugal – Portugal	1980	123	125	125	144
	1981	176	179	173	173
	1982	209	210	202	212
Spain – Espagne	1980	146	148	148	134
	1981	172	173	173	153
	1982	n.a.	n.a.	n.a.	175
Sweden – Suède	1980	122	122	122	122
	1981	135	134	134	137
	1982	147	144	144	148
Switzerland – Suisse	1980	107	106	106	108
	1981	111	110	110	115
	1982	116	114	114	121
Turkey – Turquie	1980	n.a.	n.a.	n.a.	318
	1981	n.a.	n.a.	n.a.	437
	1982	n.a.	n.a.	n.a.	580
United Kingdom – Royaume-Uni	1980	131	134	134	135
	1981	146	147	145	150
	1982	157	160	155	161
United States – Etats-Unis	1980	115	112	112	126
	1981	127	120	119	139
	1982	132	126	125	148

* Gross earnings minus income tax/Salaire brut sous déduction de l'impôt sur le revenu.

** After-tax pay minus employees' social security contributions (=disposable income)/Rémunération après impôt sous déduction des cotisations salariales de sécurité sociale (=revenu disponible).

n.a. = non available/non disponible.

1. 1977 = 100.
2. Data for 1982, however, can be found in the country table in Part III.
   On peut, cependant, trouver les données pour 1982 dans le tableau par pays de la Partie III.

Source : Country replies and, for the Consumer Price Index, Main Economic Indicators, OECD, Paris, 1983.

   Réponses par pays et, pour l'indice des prix, Principaux Indicateurs Economiques, OCDE, Paris, 1983.

Table/Tableau 2

INDICES OF GROSS EARNINGS, AFTER-TAX PAY, TAKE-HOME PAY, DISPOSABLE INCOME AND CONSUMER PRICES

INDICES DE SALAIRE BRUT, DE SALAIRE APRES IMPOT, DE REMUNERATION NETTE,

DE REVENU DISPONIBLE ET DE PRIX A LA CONSOMMATION

One-earner married couple with two children (APW)

Cas d'un couple marié avec deux enfants, ne comportant qu'un salarié (1'OM)

1982

1978 = 100

Country / Pays	Year	Gross earnings Salaire brut	After-tax pay* Salaire après impôt	Take-home pay** Rémunération nette**	Disposable income*** Revenu*** disponible	Consumer prices Prix à la consommation
Australia – Australie	1980	124	124	124	123	120
	1981	143	140	140	138	133
	1982	157	156	156	155	148
Austria – Autriche	1980	116	117	117	114	110
	1981	124	124	122	121	118
	1982	131	131	129	130	124
Belgium – Belgique	1980	115	117	117	116	112
	1981	126	125	126	125	120
	1982	129	128	128	128	130
Canada – Canada	1980	120	118	118	117	120
	1981	134	132	131	129	135
	1982	149	148	148	146	150
Denmark – Danemark	1980	124	117	116	116	123
	1981	133	125	125	124	138
	1982	149	140	138	137	152
Finland – Finlande	1980	125	123	122	122	120
	1981	141	138	138	139	134
	1982	155	152	152	153	147
France – France (2)	1980	n.a.	n.a.	n.a.	n.a.	n.a.
	1981	n.a.	n.a.	n.a.	n.a.	n.a.
	1982	n.a.	n.a.	n.a.	n.a.	n.a.
Germany – Allemagne	1980	114	114	114	114	110
	1981	119	119	118	118	116
	1982	122	122	121	120	122
Greece – Grèce (1)	1980	179	179	173	173	167
	1981	222	216	208	208	208
	1982	279	261	241	241	252
Ireland – Irlande	1980	132	131	131	132	134
	1981	155	150	149	151	161
	1982	172	170	165	168	189
	1980	149	145	144	148	13q

22

Country	Year	(1)	(2)	(3)	(4)	(5)
	1982	120	123	123	123	126
Luxembourg – Luxembourg	1980	111	118	116	116	116
	1981	120	124	123	123	122
	1982	131	133	131	131	131
Netherlands – Pays-Bas	1980	111	114	112	113	114
	1981	118	115	114	117	117
	1982	125	119	117	124	124
New Zealand – Nouvelle-Zélande	1980	135	135	132	132	137
	1981	155	146	144	144	150
	1982	179	164	162	162	177
Norway – Norvège	1980	116	113	110	112	112
	1981	132	128	123	125	123
	1982	147	142	136	139	136
Portugal – Portugal	1980	144	125	125	126	123
	1981	173	173	175	181	176
	1982	212	202	204	211	209
Spain – Espagne	1980	134	148	149	149	146
	1981	153	174	176	175	172
	1982	175	n.a.	n.a.	n.a.	n.a.
Sweden – Suède	1980	122	122	121	121	122
	1981	137	133	132	132	135
	1982	148	142	142	142	147
Switzerland – Suisse	1980	108	107	106	106	107
	1981	115	111	110	110	111
	1982	121	115	114	113	116
Turkey – Turquie	1980	318	n.a.	n.a.	n.a.	n.a.
	1981	437	n.a.	n.a.	n.a.	n.a.
	1982	580	n.a.	n.a.	n.a.	n.a.
United Kingdom – Royaume-Uni	1980	135	133	131	131	131
	1981	150	145	141	144	146
	1982	161	156	151	156	157
United States – Etats-Unis	1980	126	114	114	114	115
	1981	139	122	122	123	127
	1982	148	127	127	128	132

* Gross earnings minus income tax/salaire brut sous déduction de l'impôt sur le revenu.

** After-tax pay minus employees' social security contributions/rémunération après impôt sous déduction des cotisations salariales de sécurité sociale.

*** Take-home pay plus cash transfers/rémunération nette augmentée des transferts en espèces.

1. 1977 = 100.
2. Data for 1982, however, can be found in the country table in Part III.

On peut, cependant, trouver les données pour 1982 dans le tableau par pays de la Partie III.

Source : Country replies and, for the Consumer Price Index, Main Economic Indicators, OECD, Paris, 1983. Réponses par pays et, pour l'indice des prix, Principaux Indicateurs Economiques, OCDE, Paris, 1983.

n.a. : Not available/non disponible.

Chart 1 - *Graphique 1*

INCOME TAX PAID AS PERCENTAGE OF GROSS EARNINGS
One-earner families at the APW's wage level[1]

IMPOT SUR LE REVENU EN POURCENTAGE DU SALAIRE BRUT
Famille avec un seul salaire équivalent à celui de l'ouvrier moyen[1]

1978 - 1982

EFFECTIVE RATE OF TAX (%)

TAUX EFFECTIF D'IMPOSITION (%)

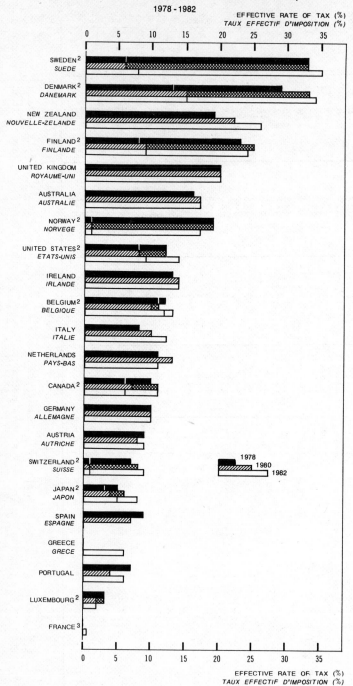

EFFECTIVE RATE OF TAX (%)

TAUX EFFECTIF D'IMPOSITION (%)

1. Countries are ranked by the rate of income tax paid in 1982, except for Spain 1980.
   Le classement des pays correspond au taux payé en 1982, saut pour l'Espagne 1980.
2. The income tax paid to central government in countries with both central and local income taxes is shown by the first post of the bar, the second section showing the other income taxes.
   Dans ces pays, des impôts locaux sont perçus. Sur le graphique la première partie de la barre représente l'impôt sur le revenu payé à l'administration centrale, la seconde les autres impôts payés.
3. Comparable figures for 1978 et 1980 are not available.
   Les chiffres comparables pour 1978 et 1980 ne sont pas disponibles.

Chart 2 - *Graphique 2*

INCOME TAX AND EMPLOYEES' SOCIAL SECURITY
CONTRIBUTIONS AS A PERCENTAGE OF GROSS EARNINGS[1]
One-earner families at APW's wage level
IMPOT SUR LE REVENU ET COTISATIONS SALARIALES
DE SECURITE SOCIALE EN POURCENTAGE DU SALAIRE BRUT[1]
Famille avec un seul salaire équivalent à celui de l'ouvrier moyen

1978 - 1982

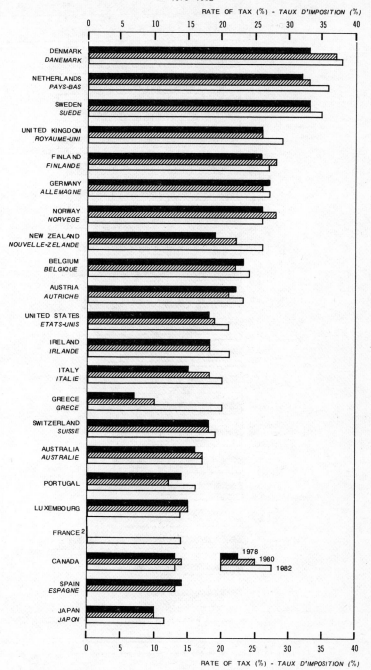

1. Countries are ranked by the 1982 figures, except for Spain 1980.
   Le classement des pays correspond au taux payé en 1982, sauf pour l'Espagne 1980.
2. Comparable figures for 1978 et 1980 are not available.
   Les chiffres comparables pour 1978 et 1980 ne sont pas disponibles.

Chart 3 - *Graphique 3*

DISPOSABLE INCOME AS PERCENTAGE OF GROSS EARNINGS[1]
One-earner families at APW's wage level

REVENU DISPONIBLE EN POURCENTAGE DU SALAIRE BRUT[1]
Un salaire par ménage, égal à celui d'un ouvrier moyen

1978 - 1982

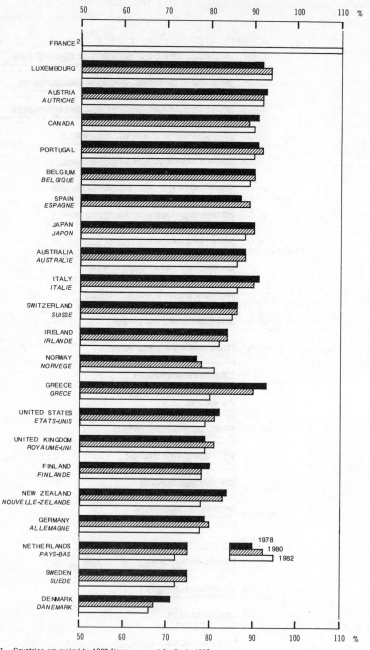

1. Countries are ranked by 1982 figures, except for Spain 1980.
    Le classement des pays correspond au taux payé en 1982, sauf pour l'Espagne 1980.
2. Comparable figures for 1978 et 1980 are not available.
    Les chiffres comparables pour 1978 et 1980 ne sont pas disponibles.

Note : Disposable income equals gross earnings minus income tax and employees' social security
    contributions paid plus cash transfers received.
    *Revenu disponible égal salaire brut moins impôts sur le revenu et cotisations salariales acquittés
    plus prestations en espèces.*

III. <u>COUNTRY TABLES/TABLEAUX PAR PAYS</u>

The following country tables, which are in a standard format, are taken from each country's reply to a questionnaire sent out in 1983, and are reproduced in their original language.

Les tableaux suivants par pays, établis selon une forme standardisée et sur la base des réponses de chaque pays à un questionnaire envoyé en 1983, sont reproduits dans leur langue originale.

THE TAX/BENEFIT POSITION OF A SINGLE PERSON AND A TWO-CHILD FAMILY
WHERE THE WIFE IS NOT WORKING

(National Currencies)

1982

Country : AUSTRALIA/AUSTRALIE

		Single person	Married couple 2 children
		(1)	(2)
1.	Annual gross earnings	17,462	17,462
2.	Income tax allowances : Lump sum deductions Married or head of family Children Social security Other		
	Total	-	-
3.	Tax credits or cash transfers included in taxable income	-	-
4.	Central government taxable income (1-2+3)	17,462	17,462
5.	Central government income tax liability (exclusive of any tax credits)	3,987	3,987
6.	Tax credits : Married or head of family Children Other	- - -	963 - -
	Total	-	963
7.	Income tax finally paid (5-6)	3,987	3,024
8.	Employees' social security contributions	-	-
9.	Additional income tax paid to political subdivisions	-	-
10.	Total payments to governments (7+8+9)	3,987	3,024
11.	Cash transfers from the government : Head of family Children	- -	- 590
	Total	-	590
12.	Disposable income (1-10+11)	13,475	15,028
13.	Disposable income as percentage of gross earnings	77.17	86.06
14.	Average rate of : - income tax paid (7+9/1) - social security paid (8/1)	22.83 -	17.32 -

*****

Social security contributions do not exist

THE TAX/BENEFIT POSITION OF A SINGLE PERSON AND A TWO-CHILD FAMILY
WHERE THE WIFE IS NOT WORKING

(National Currencies)

1982

Country : AUSTRIA/AUTRICHE

	Single person	Married couple 2 children
	(1)	(2)
1. Annual gross earnings	186,060	186,060
2. Income tax allowances :		
- tax free income (average)	13,024	13,024
- tax exemptions for christmas bonus and leave bonus	8,500	8,500
- lump sum deduction for expenses	4,914	4,914
- social security contribution (contribution to the Labour Chamber and contribution for the promotion of residential building included)	28,179	28,179
- lump sum deduction for deductible private expenses	3,276	3,276
Total	57,893	57,893
3. Tax credits or cash transfers included in taxable income	-	-
4. Taxable income (1-2+3)	128,167	128,167
5. Income tax liability (exclusive of any tax credits)		
- regular wage	27,612	27,612
- christmas & leave bonus	1,308	218
Total	28,920	27,830
6. Tax credits		
- general tax credit	4,800	4,800
- wage earners' tax credit	3,500	3,500
- single earners' tax credit	-	3,200
Total	8,300	11,500
7. Income tax finally paid (5-6)	20,620	16,330
8. Employees' social security contributions (contribution to the Labour Chamber and contribution for the promotion of residential building excluded)	26,616	26,616
9. Additional income tax paid to political subdivisions	-	-
10. Total payments to governments (7+8+9)	47,236	42,946
11. Cash transfers from the government :		
Head of family		
Children		
Total	-	28,800
12. Disposable income (1-10+11)	138,824	171,914
13. Disposable income as percentage of gross earnings	74.71	92.39
14. Average rate of :		
- income tax paid (7+9/1)	11.08	8.78
- social security paid (8/1)	14.30	14.30

Employers' social security contributions paid at this income level : 38,556

*****

SITUATION AU REGARD DE L'IMPOT ET DES TRANSFERTS SOCIAUX D'UNE PERSONNE CELIBATAIRE
ET D'UNE FAMILLE AYANT DEUX ENFANTS ET DANS LAQUELLE LA FEMME NE TRAVAILLE PAS

(Monnaies nationales)

1982

Pays : BELGIQUE

	Célibataire	Famille ayant deux enfants
1. Gain annuel brut	523.843	523.843
2. Abattement sur l'impôt sur le revenu :		
Déductions forfaitaires	53.358	53.358
Abattement au profit des personnes mariées ou des chefs de famille	-	-
Abattement au titre des enfants à charge	-	-
Sécurité sociale	56.680	56.680
Total	110.038	110.038
3. Crédits d'impôt ou prestations en espèces inclus dans le revenu imposable	-	-
4. Revenu imposable (1-2+3)	413.805	413.805
5. Impôt dû sur le revenu (sans tenir compte des crédits d'impôt)	102.170	102.170
6. Crédits d'impôt :		
Au profit des personnes mariées ou des chefs de famille	-	22.712
Au titre des enfants à charge	-	15.892
Divers	-	-
Total	-	38.604
7. Impôt sur le revenu finalement payé (5-6)	102.170	63.566
8. Cotisations de sécurité sociale des salariés	56.680	56.680
9. Impôt supplémentaire sur le revenu payé aux subdivisions politiques (*)	6.130	3.814
10. Total des paiements aux administrations (7+8+9)	164.980	124.060
11. Prestations en espèces de l'Etat :		
Au profit des chefs de famille	-	-
Au titre des enfants à charge	-	64.652
Total	-	64.652
12. Revenu disponible (1-10+11)	358.863	464.435
13. Revenu disponible en pourcentage du gain brut	68,51	88,66
14. Taux moyen :		
- de l'impôt sur le revenu versé (7+9/1)	20,67	12,86
- des cotisations de sécurité sociale versées (8/1)	10,82	10,82

(*) 6 % de l'impôt dû à l'administration centrale.

    Montant des cotisations de sécurité sociale versées par les employeurs pour ce niveau de revenu : FB 219.624 (38,82 % de 108 % du gain annuel brut).

THE TAX/BENEFIT POSITION OF A SINGLE PERSON AND A TWO-CHILD FAMILY
WHERE THE WIFE IS NOT WORKING

(National Currencies)

1982

Country : CANADA

	Single person	Married couple 2 children
	(1)	(2)
1. Annual gross earnings	22,067	22,067
2. Income tax allowances :		
Lump sum deductions	3,660	3,660
Married or head of family	0	3,110
Children	0	1,340
Social security	568	568
General employment expense	500	500
Total	4,728	9,178
3. Tax credits or cash transfers included in taxable income	-	646
4. Taxable income (1-2+3)	17,339	13,535
5. Income tax liability (exclusive of any tax credits)	2,965	1,951
6. Tax credits :		
Married or head of family	-	-
Children	-	686
Other	-	-
Total	-	686
7. Income tax finally paid (5-6)	2,965	1,265
8. Employees' social security contributions	568	568
9. Additional income tax paid to political subdivisions (*).	1,488	1,105
10. Total payments to governments (7+8+9)	5,021	2,938
11. Cash transfers from the government :		
Head of family	-	-
Children	-	646
Total	-	646
12. Disposable income (1-10+11)	17,046	19,775
13. Disposable income as percentage of gross earnings	77.25	89.61
14. Average rate of :		
- income tax paid (7+9/1)	20.18	10.74
- social security paid (8/1)	2.57	2.57

(*) As rates vary, a weighted average of the provincial rates, i.e. 47 per cent of basic federal tax, is applied.

*****

Employers' social security contributions paid at this income level : $

31

THE TAX/BENEFIT POSITION OF A SINGLE PERSON AND A TWO-CHILD FAMILY
WHERE THE WIFE IS NOT WORKING

(National Currencies)

1982

Country : DENMARK/DANEMARK

	Single person	Married couple 2 children
	(1)	(2)
1. Annual gross earnings	141,200	141,200
2. Income tax allowances :		
Lump sum deductions	-	-
Married or head of family	-	-
Children	-	-
Social security	-	-
Other : Standard deduction for wage and salary earners	3,200	3,200
Total	3,200	3,200
3. Tax credits or cash transfers included in taxable income	-	-
4. Taxable income (1-2+3)	138,000	138,000
5. Income tax liability (exclusive of any tax credits)	25,992	25,992
6. Tax credits :		
Married or head of family	-	-
Children	-	-
Other : Personal tax deduction	2,506	5,011
Total	2,506	5,011
7. Income tax finally paid (5-6)	23,486	20,981
8. Employees' social security contributions	6,377	5,594
9. Additional income tax paid to political subdivision (*)	30,874	26,419
10. Total payments to governments (7+8+9)	60,737	52,994
11. Cash transfers from the government :		
Head of family	-	-
Children	-	4,368
Total	-	4,368
12. Disposable income (1-10+11)	80,463	92,574
13. Disposable income as percentage of gross earnings	56.99	65.56
14. Average rate of :		
- income tax paid (7+9/1)	38.50	33.57
- social security paid (8/1)	4.52	3.96

(*) As rates vary, the average 25.6 % is applied.

*****

Employers' social security contributions paid at this income level : Kr. 633

THE TAX/BENEFIT POSITION OF A SINGLE PERSON AND A TWO-CHILD FAMILY
WHERE THE WIFE IS NOT WORKING

(National Currencies)

1982

Country : FINLAND/FINLANDE

		Single person	Married couple 2 children
		(1)	(2)
1.	Annual gross earnings	58,229	58,229
2.	Income tax allowances :		
	Basic deduction of earned income	9,000	9,000
	Spouse deduction	-	4,500
	Deduction of earned income	1,000	1,000
	Standard deduction for wage-earners	572	572
	Total	10,572	15,072
3.	Tax credits or cash transfers included in taxable income	-	-
4.	Taxable income (1-2+3)	47,657	43,157
5.	Income tax liability (exclusive of any tax credits)	8,129	6,824
6.	Tax credits :		
	Children	-	1,400
7.	Income tax finally paid (5-6)	8,129	5,424
8.	Employees' social security contributions	1,613	1,543
9.	Any additional income tax due to political subdivision (*)		
	Local income tax	8,584	8,209
	Church tax	572	547
	Total	9,156	8,756
10.	Total payments to governments (7+8+9)	18,898	15,723
11.	Cash transfers from the government :		
	Children	-	3,196
12.	Disposable income (1-10+11)	39,331	45,702
13.	Disposable income as percentage of gross earnings	67.54	78.49
14.	Average rate of :		
	- income tax paid (7+9/1)	29.68	24.35
	- social security paid (8/1)	2.77	2.65

(*) As rates vary a typical cas is applied, i.e. Helsinki

*****

Employers' social security contribution paid at this income level : Fmk. 3,668

SITUATION AU REGARD DE L'IMPOT ET DES TRANSFERTS SOCIAUX D'UNE PERSONNE CELIBATAIRE ET D'UNE FAMILLE AYANT DEUX ENFANTS ET DANS LAQUELLE LA FEMME NE TRAVAILLE PAS

(Monnaies nationales)

1982

Pays : FRANCE

	Célibataire	Famille ayant deux enfants
	(1)	(2)
1. Gain annuel brut	68.735	68.735
2. Abattements sur l'impôt sur le revenu de l'administration centrale :		
Abattement de base	10.775	10.775
Abattement au profit des personnes mariées ou des chefs de famille	-	-
Abattements pour enfants à charge	-	-
Sécurité sociale	8.890	8.890
Impôts sur le revenu des administrations non centrales	-	-
Dépenses professionnelles	5.985	5.985
Divers	-	-
Total	25.650	25.650
3. Crédits d'impôts ou prestations en espèces inclus dans le revenu imposable de l'administration centrale	-	-
4. Revenu imposable de l'administration centrale (1-2+3)	43.085	43.085
5. Impôt sur le revenu dû à l'administration centrale (non compris les crédits d'impôts)	6.020	430
6. Crédits d'impôts :		
Au profit des personnes mariées ou des chefs de famille	-	-
Pour enfants à charge	-	-
Divers	-	-
Total	-	-
7. Impôt sur le revenu finalement payé (5-6)	6.020	430
8. Cotisations de sécurité sociale des salariés	8.890	8.890
9. Impôt supplémentaire sur le revenu payé aux subdivisions politiques	-	-
10. Total des paiements aux administrations publiques (7+8+9)	14.910	9.320
11. Prestations en espèces des administrations publiques :		
Au profit des chefs de famille		-
Au titre de deux enfants à charge		16.010
Total		16.010
12. Revenu disponible (1-10+11)	53.825	75.425
13. Revenu disponible en pourcentage du gain brut (12/1)	78,31	109,73
14. Taux moyen :		
- de l'impôt sur le revenu versé (7+9/1)	8,76	0,63
- des cotisations de sécurité sociale versées par les salariés (8/1)	12,93	12,93

THE TAX/BENEFIT POSITION OF A SINGLE PERSON AND A TWO-CHILD FAMILY
WHERE THE WIFE IS NOT WORKING

(National Currencies)

1982

Country : GERMANY/ALLEMAGNE

	Single person	Married couple 2 children
	(1)	(2)
1. Annual gross earnings	36,201	36,201
2. Central government income tax allowances :		
Basic allowance	1,080	1,080
Married or head of family	–	–
Children	–	1,200
Social security	3,510	5,994
Income taxes of non-central government	–	–
Work-related expenses	564	564
Other tax-free income	1,086	1,086
Church-tax	570	540
Total	6,810	10,464
3. Tax credits or cash transfers included in Central government taxable income	–	–
4. Central government taxable income (1-2+3)	29,391	25,737
5. Central government income tax liability (exclusive of any tax credits)	6,332	3,802
6. Tax credits :		
Married or head of family	–	–
Children	–	–
Other	–	–
Total	–	–
7. Income tax finally paid (5-6)	6,332	3,802
8. Employees' social security contributions	5,969	5,969
9. Additional income tax paid to political subdivisions	–	–
10. Total payments to general governments (7+8+9)	12,301	9,771
11. Cash transfers from general government :		
For head of family	–	–
For two children	–	1,800
Total	–	1,800
12. Disposable income (1-10+11)	23,900	28,230
13. Disposable income as percentage of gross earnings	66.02	77.98
14. Average rate of :		
- Income tax paid (7+9/1)	17.49	10.50
- Employees' social security paid (8/1)	16.49	16.49

Employer's social security contributions paid at this income level : DM 5,969

THE TAX/BENEFIT POSITION OF A SINGLE PERSON AND A TWO-CHILD FAMILY
WHERE THE WIFE IS NOT WORKING

(National Currencies)

1982

Country : GREECE/GRECE

	Single person	Married couple 2 children
	(1)	(2)
1. Annual gross earnings	469,196	469,196
2. Central government income tax allowances :		
Basic allowance	20,000	20,000
Married or head of family	-	20,000
Children	-	30,000
Social security	62,168	62,168
Income taxes of non-central government	-	-
Work-related expenses		
Other	131,960	131,960
Total	214,128	264,128
3. Cash transfers included in Central government taxable income	-	93,839
4. Central government taxable income (1-2+3)	255,068	298,907
5. Central government income tax liability (exclusive of any tax credits)	27,094	49,186
6. Tax credits :		
Married or head of family	-	4,800
Children	-	14,500
Other	-	-
Total	-	19,300
7. Income tax finally paid (5-6)	27,094	29,886
8. Employees' social security contributions	62,168	62,168
9. Additional income tax paid to political subdivisions	-	-
10. Total payments to general governments (7+8+9)	89,262	92,054
11. Cash transfers from general government :		
For head of family	-	-
For two children	-	-
Total	-	-
12. Disposable income (1-10+11)	379,934	377,142
13. Disposable income as percentage of gross earnings	80.98	80.38
14. Average rate of :		
- Income tax paid (7+9/1)	5.77	6.37
- Employees' social security paid (8/1)	13.25	13.25

Employer's compulsory social security contributions paid at this income level : Dzs 102,050
(at a rate of 21.75 %)

THE TAX/BENEFIT POSITION OF A SINGLE PERSON AND A TWO-CHILD FAMILY
WHERE THE WIFE IS NOT WORKING

(National Currencies)

1982

Country : IRELAND/IRLANDE

		Single person	Married couple 2 children
		(1)	(2)
1.	Annual gross earnings	7,652	7,652
2.	Central government income tax allowances :		
	Basic allowance	1,450	–
	Married or head of family	–	2,900
	Children	–	200
	Social security	312	312
	Income taxes of non-central government	–	–
	Work-related expenses	600	600
	Other (Employee allowance)	–	–
	Total	2,362	4,012
3.	Tax credits or cash transfers included in Central government taxable income	–	–
4.	Central government taxable income (1-2+3)	5,290	3,640
5.	Central government income tax liability (exclusive of any tax credits)	1,880.50	1,074
6.	Tax credits :		
	Married or head of family	–	–
	Children	–	–
	Other	–	–
	Total	–	–
7.	Income tax finally paid (5-6)	1,880.50	1,074
8.	Employees' social security contributions	517.23	517.23
9.	Additional income tax paid to political subdivisions	–	–
10.	Total payments to general governments (7+8+9)	2,397.73	1,591.23
11.	Cash transfers from general government :		
	For head of family	–	–
	For two children	–	247.50
	Total	–	247.50
12.	Disposable income (1-10+11)	5,254.27	6,308.27
13.	Disposable income as percentage of gross earnings (12/1)	68.67	82.44
14.	Average rate of :		
	- Income tax paid (7+9/1)	24.58	14.04
	- Employees' social security paid (8/1)	6.76	6.76

Employer's compulsory social security contributions paid at this income level : £856.24

SITUATION AU REGARD DE L'IMPOT ET DES TRANSFERTS SOCIAUX D'UNE PERSONNE CELIBATAIRE ET
D'UNE FAMILLE AYANT DEUX ENFANTS ET DANS LAQUELLE LA FEMME NE TRAVAILLE PAS

(Monnaies nationales)

1982

Pays : ITALIE/ITALY

	Célibataire	Famille ayant deux enfants
	(1)	(2)
1. Gain annuel brut	11.447.520	11.447.520
2. Abattements sur l'impôt sur le revenu de l'administration centrale :		
Abattement de base	–	–
Abattement au profit des personnes mariées ou des chefs de famille	–	–
Abattements pour enfants à charge	–	–
Sécurité sociale	990.210	990.210
Impôts sur le revenu des administrations non centrales	–	–
Dépenses professionnelles	–	–
Divers	–	–
Total	990.210	990.210
3. Crédits d'impôts ou prestations en espèces inclus dans le revenu imposable de l'administration	–	–
4. Revenu imposable de l'administration centrale (1-2+3)	10.457.310	10.457.310
5. Impôt sur le revenu dû à l'administration centrale (non compris les crédits d'impôts)	1.878.473	1.878.473
6. Crédits d'impôts :		
Crédit personnel	36.000	36.000
Au profit des personnes mariées ou des chefs de famille	–	180.000
Pour enfants à charge	–	72.000
Divers (dépenses pour la production du revenu)	240.000	240.000
Total	276.000	528.000
7. Impôt sur le revenu finalement payé (5-6)	1.602.473	1.350.473
8. Cotisations de sécurité sociale des salariés	990.210	990.210
9. Impôt supplémentaire sur le revenu payé aux subdivisions politiques	–	–
10. Total des paiements aux administrations publiques (7+8+9)	2.592.683	2.340.683
11. Prestations en espèces des administrations publiques :		
Au profit des chefs de famille	–	233.580
Au titre de deux enfants à charge	–	467.160
Total	–	700.740
12. Revenu disponible (1-10+11)	8.854.837	9.807.577
13. Revenu disponible en pourcentage du gain brut	77,35	85,67
14. Taux moyen :		
- de l'impôt sur le revenu versé (7+9/1)	13,99	11,79
- des cotisations de sécurité sociale versées par les salariés (8/1)	8,65	8,65

Montant des cotisations de sécurité sociale versées par les employeurs pour ce niveau de revenu : - Entreprises de plus de 50 travailleurs dépendants : 45,93 % = 5.527.845 du gain annuel brut,
     - Entreprises de moins de 50 travailleurs dépendants: 45,65 % = 5.225.792 du gain annuel brut.

THE TAX/BENEFIT POSITION OF A SINGLE PERSON AND A TWO-CHILD FAMILY
WHERE THE WIFE IS NOT WORKING

(National Currencies)

1982

Country : JAPAN/JAPON

	Single person	Married couple 2 children
	(1)	(2)
1. Annual gross earnings	4,258,600	4,258,600
2. Central government income tax allowances :		
Basic allowance	1,301,720	1,301,720
Married or head of family	290,000	580,000
Children	-	580,000
Social security	165,172	165,172
Income taxes of non-central government	-	-
Work-related expenses	-	-
Other	-	-
Total	1,756,892	2,626,892
3. Tax credits or cash transfers included in Central government taxable income	-	-
4. Central government taxable income (1-2+3)	2,501,708	1,631,708
5. Central government income tax liability (exclusive of any tax credits)	330,307	192,439
6. Tax credits :		
Married or head of family	-	-
Children	-	-
Other	-	-
Total	-	-
7. Income tax finally paid (5-6)	330,307	192,439
8. Employees' social security contributions	165,172	165,172
9. Additional income tax paid to political subdivisions	206,134	132,023
10. Total payments to general governments (7+8+9)	701,613	489,634
11. Cash transfers from general government :		
For head of family	-	-
For two children	-	-
Total	-	-
12. Disposable income (1-10+11)	3,556,987	3,768,966
13. Disposable income as percentage of gross earnings (12/1)	83.52	88.50
14. Average rate of :		
- Income tax paid (7+9/1)	12.60	7.62
- Employees' social security paid (8/1)	3.88	3.88

Employer's compulsory social security contributions paid at this income level : Yen 172,891

SITUATION AU REGARD DE L'IMPOT ET DES TRANSFERTS SOCIAUX D'UNE PERSONNE CELIBATAIRE ET
D'UNE FAMILLE AYANT DEUX ENFANTS ET DANS LAQUELLE LA FEMME NE TRAVAILLE PAS

(Monnaies nationales)

1982

Pays : LUXEMBOURG

	Célibataire	Famille ayant deux enfants
	(1)	(2)
1. Gain annuel brut	558.200	558.200
2. Abattements sur l'impôt sur le revenu de l'administration centrale :		
Abattement de base	36.000	36.000
Abattement au profit des personnes mariées ou des chefs de famille	-	-
Abattements pour enfants à charge	-	-
Sécurité sociale	66.984	66.984
Impôts sur le revenu des administrations non centrales	-	-
Dépenses professionnelles	-	-
Divers (Abattement compensatoire)	18.000	18.000
Total	120.984	120.984
3. Crédits d'impôts ou prestations en espèces inclus dans le revenu imposable de l'administration centrale	-	-
4. Revenu imposable de l'administration centrale (1-2+3)	437.216	437.216
5. Impôt sur le revenu dû à l'administration centrale (non compris les crédits d'impôts)	87.906	13.036
6. Crédits d'impôts :		
Au profit des personnes mariées ou des chefs de famille	-	-
Pour enfants à charge	-	-
Divers	-	-
Total	-	-
7. Impôt sur le revenu finalement payé (5-6)	87.906	13.036
8. Cotisations de sécurité sociale des salariés	66.984	66.984
9. Impôt supplémentaire sur le revenu payé aux subdivisions politiques	-	-
9a Impôt de solidarité	4.395	651
10. Total des paiements aux administrations publiques (7+8+9)	159.285	80.671
11. Prestations en espèces des administrations publiques :		
- Au profit des chefs de famille	-	-
- Au titre de deux enfants à charge	-	45.648
Total	-	45.648
12. Revenu disponible (1-10+11)	398.915	523.177
13. Revenu disponible en pourcentage du gain brut (12/1)	71.46	93.73
14. Taux moyen :		
- de l'impôt sur le revenu versé (7+9/1)	16,54	2,45
- des cotisations de sécurité sociale versées par les salariés (8/1)	12,00	12,00

Montant des cotisations obligatoires de sécurité sociale versées par les employeurs pour ce
niveau de revenu : L.Frs.85.400

THE TAX/BENEFIT POSITION OF A SINGLE PERSON AND A TWO-CHILD FAMILY
WHERE THE WIFE IS NOT WORKING

(National currencies)

1982

Country : NETHERLANDS/PAYS-BAS

	Single person ≥35 years	Married couple 2 children
	(1)	(2)
1. Annual gross earnings	38,870	38,870
2. Income tax allowances :		
a. contribution pension scheme	777	777
b. sickness, infirmity and unemployment	3,343	3,343
c. lump sum for deductible expenses	1,000	1,000
d. premium general old age pension and widow's and orphans' benefits	4,430	4,430
e. personal : single person	9,423	-
f. personal : married man	-	12,078
g. personal : working wife	-	-
h. children	-	-
Total	18,973	21,628
3. Employers health insurance contribution included in taxable income	1,686	1,686
4. Taxable income (1-2+3)	21,583	18,928
5. Income tax liability	-	-
6. Tax credits	-	-
7. Income tax finally paid	5,221	4,351
8. Employees' social security contributions (*)	9,459	9,459
9. Additional income tax paid to political subdivisions	-	-
10. Total payments to the government (7+8)	14,680	13,810
11. Cash transfers from the government	-	3,016
12. Disposable income (1-10+11)	24,190	28,076
13. Disposable income as percentage of gross earnings	62.23	72.23
14. Average rate of :		
- income tax paid (7:1)	13.43	11.19
- social security paid (8:1)	24.34	24.34

*) Private pension contribution (2a) excluded.

Employees' health insurance contribution (equal to 3) included.

Employer's social security contributions paid at this income level : Dfl. 9,172

THE TAX/BENEFIT POSITION OF A SINGLE PERSON AND A TWO-CHILD FAMILY
WHERE THE WIFE IS NOT WORKING

(National Currencies)

1982

Country : NEW ZEALAND/NOUVELLE-ZELANDE

	Single person	Married couple 2 children
	(1)	(2)
1. Annual gross earnings	15,952.05	15,952.05
2. Central government income tax allowances :		
Basic allowance - Standard Allowance	52.00	52.00
Married or head of family	-	-
Children	-	-
Social security	-	-
Income taxes of non-central government	-	-
Work-related expenses	-	-
Other	-	-
Total	52.00	52.00
3. Tax credits or cash transfers included in Central government taxable income	-	-
4. Central government taxable income (1-2+3)	15,900.05	15,900.05
5. Central government income tax liability (exclusive of any tax credits)	4,567.75	4,567.75
6. Tax credits :		
Married or head of family	-	78.00
Yourng Family Rebate	-	102.00
Other Family Rebate	-	244.50
Total	-	424.50
7. Income tax finally paid (5-6)	4,567.75	4,143.25
8. Employees' social security contributions	-	-
9. Additional income tax paid to political subdivisions	-	-
10. Total payments to general governments (7+8+9)	4,567.75	4,143.25
11. Cash transfers from general government :		
For head of family	-	-
For two children - Family Benefit	-	624.00
12. Disposable income (1-10+11)	11,384.30	12,432.80
13. Disposable income as percentage of gross earnings	71.37	77.94
14. Average rate of :		
Income tax paid (7+9/1)	28.63	25.97
Employees' social security paid (8/1)	-	-

π Family benefit of $6.00 weekly per child is paid to the mother in the normal family situation ; to the father if he is a solo parent.

* Young family rebate allowable where there is a child under 5 years and the income of the principal income earner is under $17,600 if the income under $13,700 the rebate is $234, between $13,700 and $17,600 the rebate reduces by 6 cents in the dollar for each dollar in excess of $13,700.

*****

Employers' social security contributions paid at this income level : zero.

+ Low Income Family Rebate of $234 allowable to the principal income earner where there is a child for whom the family benefit is payable and the combined incomes of the spouses is less than $9,800. The rebate diminishes by 6 cents for each complete dollar of the excess income of the spouses, or a solo parent where the excess income is over $9,800.

THE TAX/BENEFIT POSITION OF A SINGLE PERSON AND A TWO-CHILD FAMILY
WHERE THE WIFE IS NOT WORKING

(National Currencies)

1982

Country : NORWAY/NORVEGE

	Single person	Married couple 2 children
	(1)	(2)
1. Annual gross earnings	103,150	103,150
2. Central government income tax allowances :		
Basic allowance	-	-
Married or head of family	-	-
Children	-	-
Social security	-	-
Income taxes of non-central government	-	
Work-related expenses	3,100	3,100
Other	700	700
Total	3,800	3,800
3. Tax credits or cash transfers included in Central government taxable income	-	-
4. Central government taxable income (1-2+3)	99,350	99,350
5. Central government income tax liability (exclusive of any tax credits)	5,931	2,149
6. Tax credits :		
Married or head of family	-	-
Children	-	2,000
Other	825	825
Total	825	2,825
7. Income tax finally paid (5-6)	5,106	- 676
8. Employees' social security contributions	9,833	9,415
9. Additional income tax paid to political subdivisions	20,665	18,480
10. Total payments to general governments (7+8+9)	35,604	27,219
11. Cash transfers from general government :		
For head of family	-	-
For two children	-	7,260
Total	-	7,260
12. Disposable income (1-10+11)	67,546	83,191
13. Disposable income as percentage of gross earnings	65.48	80.65
14. Average rate of :		
- Income tax paid (7+9/1)	24.99	17.26
- Employees' social security paid (8/1)	9.53	9.13

Employers' compulsory social security contributions paid at this income level : Kr. 16,813

SITUATION AU REGARD DE L'IMPOT ET DES TRANSFERTS SOCIAUX D'UNE PERSONNE CELIBATAIRE ET
D'UNE FAMILLE AYANT DEUX ENFANTS ET DANS LAQUELLE LA FEMME NE TRAVAILLE PAS

(monnaies nationales)

1982

Pays : PORTUGAL

	Célibataire	Famille ayant deux enfants
	(1)	(2)
1. Gain annuel brut	234.720**	234.720**
2. Abattements sur l'impôt sur le revenu de l'administration centrale		
Abattement au profit du contribuable	100.000	-
Abattement au profit du contribuable et conjoint	-	150.000
Déduction de 30 % sur les revenus du contribuable (max. Esc. 50.000)	50.000	50.000
Déduction de 30 % sur les revenus du conjoint (max. Esc. 50.000)	-	-
Impôt Professionnel	14.084	14.084
Cotisation de Sécurité Sociale	18.778	18.778
Cotisation pour le Fonds de Chômage	5.868	5.868
Abattement au titre des enfants à charge	-	40.000
Total	188.730	278.730
3. Crédits d'impôt ou prestations en espèces inclus dans le revenu imposable	-	-
4. Revenu imposable de l'administration centrale (1-2+3)	45.990	-
5. Impôt dû sur le revenu de l'administration centrale (sans tenir compte des crédits d'impôt) a) b)	a) 14.084 b) 1.840	14.084
6. Crédits d'impôt :		
Au profit des personnes mariées ou des chefs de famille	-	-
Au titre des enfants à charge	-	-
Divers	-	-
Total	-	-
7. Impôt sur le revenu finalement payé (5-6)	15.924	14.084
8. Cotisations de sécurité sociale des salariés	18.778	18.778
Cotisation pour le fonds de chômage (2,5% du gain annuel brut)	5.868	5.868
9. Impôt supplémentaire sur le revenu payé aux subdivisions politiques	-	-
10. Total des paiements aux administrations (7+8+9)	40.570	38.730
11. Prestations en espèces des administrations publiques		
Au profit des chefs de famille	-	-
Au titre des enfants à charge	-	9.800
Total	-	9.800
12. Revenu disponible (1-10+11)	194.150	205.790
13. Revenu disponible en pourcentage du gain brut (12/1)	82,72	87,67
14. Taux moyen :		
- de l'impôt sur le revenu versé (7+9/1)	6,78	6,00
- des cotisations de sécurité sociale versées par les salariés (8/1)	10,50	10,50

** Estimation.

a) Impôt Professionnel qui frappe le gain annuel brut.
b) Impôt Complémentaire qui frappe le revenu imposable.

Note : L'Impôt Complémentaire sera payé au cours de l'année suivant celle à laquelle le revenu
se rapporte.

Le montant des cotisations de sécurité sociale versées par les employeurs pour ce niveau de
revenu : Esc. 49.292

SITUATION AU REGARD DE L'IMPOT ET DES TRANSFERTS SOCIAUX D'UNE PERSONNE CELIBATAIRE ET
D'UNE FAMILLE AYANT DEUX ENFANTS ET DANS LAQUELLE LA FEMME NE TRAVAILLE PAS

(monnaies nationales)

1982

Pays : ESPAGNE/SPAIN

	Célibataire	Famille ayant deux enfants
	(1)	(2)
1. Gain annuel brut		
2. Abattements sur l'impôt sur le revenu : Déductions forfaitaires Abattement au profit des personnes mariées ou des chefs de famille Abattement au titre des enfants à charge Sécurité sociale Divers		
Total		
3. Crédits d'impôt ou prestations en espèces inclus dans le revenu imposable		
4. Revenu imposable (1-2+3)		
5. Impôt dû sur le revenu		
6. Crédits d'impôt : Au profit des personnes mariées ou des chefs de famille Au titre des enfants à charge Divers		
Total		
7. Impôt sur le revenu finalement payé (5-6)		
8. Cotisations de sécurité sociale des salariés		
9. Impôt supplémentaire sur le revenu payé aux subdivisions politiques (*)		
10. Total des paiements aux administrations (7+8+9)		
11. Prestations en espèces de l'Etat :		
12. Revenu disponible (1-10+11)		
13. Revenu disponible en pourcentage du gain brut		
14. Taux moyen : - de l'impôt sur le revenu versé (7+9/1) - des cotisations de sécurité sociale versées (8/1)		

Montant des cotisations de sécurité sociale versées par les employeurs pour ce niveau de revenu :

THE TAX/BENEFIT POSITION OF A SINGLE PERSON AND A TWO-CHILD FAMILY
WHERE THE WIFE IS NOT WORKING

(National Currencies)

1982

Country : SWEDEN/SUEDE

		Single person	Married couple 2 children
		(1)	(2)
1.	Annual gross earnings	84,600	84,600
2.	Central government income tax allowances :		
	Basic allowance	-	-
	Married or head of family	-	-
	Children	-	-
	Social security	-	-
	Income taxes of non-central government	-	-
	Work-related expenses	-	-
	Other	100	100
	Total	100	100
3.	Tax credits or cash transfers included in Central government taxable income	-	-
4.	Central government taxable income (1-2+3)	84,500	84,500
5.	Central government income tax liability (exclusive of any tax credits)	8,497	8,497
6.	Tax credits :		
	Married or head of family	-	1,800
	Children	-	-
	Other	-	-
	Total	-	1,800
7.	Income tax finally paid (5-6)	8,497	6,697
8.	Employees' social security contributions	-	-
9.	Additional income tax paid to political subdivisions	22,900	22,900
10.	Total payments to general governments (7+8+9)	31,397	29,597
11.	Cash transfers from general government :		
	For head of family	-	-
	For two children	-	6,000
	Total	-	6,000
12.	Disposable income (1-10+11)	53,203	61,003
13.	Disposable income as percentage of gross earnings	62.89	72.11
14.	Average rate of :		
	Income tax paid (7+9/1)	37.11	34.98
	Employees' social security paid (8/1)	-	-

* As rates vary, the average 29.74 per cent is applied.

Employers' social security contributions paid at this income level : k. 23,984

SITUATION AU REGARD DE L'IMPOT ET DES TRANSFERTS SOCIAUX D'UNE PERSONNE CELIBATAIRE ET

D'UNE FAMILLE AYANT DEUX ENFANTS ET DANS LAQUELLE LA FEMME NE TRAVAILLE PAS

(monnaies nationales)

1982

Pays : SUISSE/SWITZERLAND

	Célibataire	Famille ayant deux enfants
	(1)	(2)
1. Gain annuel brut	40.100	40.100
2. Abattements sur l'impôt sur le revenu de l'administration centrale :		
Abattement de base	-	-
Abattement au profit des personnes mariées ou des chefs de famille	-	2.500
Abattements pour enfants à charge	-	2.400
Sécurité sociale AVS 5 % ; AC Q 15 % ; max. 70	2.065	2.065
Impôts sur le revenu des administrations non centrales	-	-
Dépenses professionnelles	1.200	1.200
Divers (5 %, max. 2.000)	2.000	2.000
Total	5.265	10.165
3. Crédits d'impôts ou prestations en espèces inclus dans le revenu imposable de l'administration centrale	-	1.680
4. Revenu imposable de l'administration centrale (1-2+3)	34.835	31.615
5. Impôt sur le revenu dû à l'administration centrale (non compris les crédits d'impôts)	580	410
6. Crédits d'impôts :		
Au profit des personnes mariées ou des chefs de famille	-	-
Au titre des enfants à charge	-	-
Divers	-	-
Total	-	-
7. Impôt sur le revenu finalement payé (5-6)	580	410
8. Cotisations de sécurité sociale des salariés		
AVS/AC	2.065	2.065
Pension	2.005	2.089
9. Impôt supplémentaire sur le revenu payé aux subdivisions politiques	4.782	3.088
10. Total des paiements aux administrations publiques (7+8+9)	9.432	7.652
11. Prestations en espèces des administrations publiques :		
Au profit des chefs de famille	-	-
Au titre de deux enfants à charge	-	1.680
Total	-	1.680
12. Revenu disponible (1-10+11)	30.668	34.128
13. Revenu disponible en pourcentage du gain brut	76,47	85,11
14. Taux moyen :		
- de l'impôt sur le revenu versé (7+9/1)	13,37	8,72
- des cotisations de sécurité sociale versées par les salariés (8/1)	10,15	10,36

Les cotisations de sécurité sociale supérieures à 10,2 % sont dues au fait que les cotisations d'assurance-vieillesse publique et d'assurance-chômage (5,15 % du salaire brut, non comprises les prestations en espèces pour enfants à charge) et les cotisations pour pensions privées (5 % du salaire brut plus prestations en espèces pour enfants à charge) sont calculées ici sur les salaires bruts, prestations pour enfants à charge non comprises.

Cotisations obligatoires de sécurité sociale pour ce niveau de revenu : 10,2 %

THE TAX/BENEFIT POSITION OF A SINGLE PERSON AND A TWO-CHILD FAMILY
WHERE THE WIFE IS NOT WORKING

(National Currencies)

1982

Country : UNITED KINGDOM/ROYAUME-UNI

	Single person	Married couple 2 children
	(1)	(2)
1. Annual gross earnings	7,467	7,467
2. Central government income tax allowances :		
Basic allowance	1,565	1,565
Married or head of family	-	880
Children	-	-
Social security	-	-
Income taxes of non-central government	-	-
Work-related expenses	-	-
Other	-	-
Total	1,565	2,445
3. Tax credits or cash transfers included in Central government taxable income	-	-
4. Central government taxable income (1-2+3)	5,902	5,022
5. Central government income tax liability (exclusive of any tax credits)	1,771	1,507
6. Tax credits :		
Married or head of family	-	-
Children	-	-
Other	-	-
Total	-	-
7. Income tax finally paid (5-6)	1,771	1,507
8. Employees' social security contributions	653	653
9. Additional income tax paid to political subdivisions	-	-
10. Total payments to general governments (7+8+9)	2,424	2,160
11. Cash transfers from general government :		
For head of family	-	-
For two children	-	569
Total	-	569
12. Disposable income (1-10+11)	5,043	5,876
13. Disposable income as percentage of gross earnings	67.54	78.69
14. Average rate of :		
- Income tax paid (7+9/1)	23.71	20.18
- Employees' social security paid (8/1)	8.75	8.75

The employers' compulsory social security contributions paid at this income level :£910

THE TAX/BENEFIT POSITION OF A SINGLE PERSON AND A TWO-CHILD FAMILY
WHERE THE WIFE IS NOT WORKING

(National Currencies)

1982

Country : UNITED STATES/ETATS-UNIS

	Single person	Married couple 2 children
	(1)	(2)
1. Annual gross earnings	17,136	17,136
2. Central government income tax allowances :		
Basic allowance	3,300	5,400
Married or head of family	-	-
Children	-	2,000
Social security	-	-
Income taxes of non-central government	-	-
Work-related expenses	-	-
Other	-	-
Total	3,300	7,400
3. Tax credits or cash transfers included in Central government taxable income	-	-
4. Central government taxable income (1-2+3)	13,836	9,736
5. Central government income tax liability (exclusive of any tax credits)	2,637	1,469
6. Tax credits :		
Married or head of family	-	-
Children	-	-
Other	-	-
Total	-	-
7. Income tax finally paid (5-6)	2,637	1,469
8. Employees' social security contributions	1,148	1,148
9. Additional income tax paid to political subdivisions (*)		
Michigan	755	528
Detroit	496	442
10. Total payments to general governments (7+8+9)	5,036	3,587
11. Cash transfers from general government :		
For head of family	-	-
For two children	-	-
Total	-	-
12. Disposable income (1-10+11)	12,100	13,549
13. Disposable income as percentage of gross earnings	70.61	79.07
14. Average rate of :		
- Income tax paid (7+9/1)	22.69	14.23
- Employees' social security paid (8/1)	6.70	6.70

*) As rates vary, the data refer to local taxes in Detroit, Michigan which could be considered to be a typical case.

*****

Employers' social security contributions paid at this income level : $ 1,148

IV. DESCRIPTION OF THE TAX/BENEFIT SYSTEMS

DESCRIPTION DES SYSTEMES D'IMPOTS ET DE TRANSFERTS SOCIAUX

The following country chapters, which are in a standard format, are reproduced in the original language.

Les chapitres par pays ci-après, présentés dans un format normalisé, sont reproduits dans leur langue originale.

AUSTRALIA(1)

1. INCOME TAX

a) Tax Unit

Members of the family are taxed separately.

b) Tax Allowances and Tax Credits

Net tax payable is arrived at after reducing the gross tax by dependant rebates and any other rebates to which the taxpayer may be entitled.

Marriage

A rebate for a spouse of Aus.$830(*) is allowable provided that the spouse's income does not exceed Aus.$282. The rebate is reduced by Aus.$1 for every Aus.$4 by which the spouse's separate net income exceeds Aus.$282.

* Aus.$963 where there is a dependent child.

Children

No tax rebates for maintenance of children. Cash transfers (family allowances) generally paid to mother.

c) Income Tax Schedule

2. SOCIAL SECURITY CONTRIBUTIONS

No contributions.

3. CASH TRANSFERS

a) Amount for marriage

None.

---

1. Annual equivalent of wages paid in November 1982 to adult male workers (non-managerial) in manufacturing industry was Aus.$17,462. This has been taken as the annual gross earnings for 1982-83.

b) Amount for children (generally paid to mother)

   (1982-83 financial year); monthly rates:

Aus.$

	Prior to November 1982	From November 1982
First child	15.20	22.80
Second child	21.70	32.55
Third child	39.00	39.00
Fourth child	39.00	39.00
Fifth and later children	45.55	45.55
Child in an institution	39.00	39.00

4. EFFECT ON TAX AND CASH TRANSFERS WHEN THE WIFE WORKS

a) On husband's allowances and transfers

   Allowance for spouse is reduced or lost (depending on amount of income received, see 1. Marriage).

b) Special treatment for wife

   None.

5. MAIN CHANGES SINCE 1982

General rates of tax - resident individuals 1982-83
In Aus.$

Total taxable income

Not less than	Not more than	Tax at general rates on total taxable income
0	4,462	nil
4,462	17,894	nil + 30.67¢ for each $1 in excess of 4,462
17,894	19,500	4,119.5,944 + 35.33¢ for each $1 in excess of 17,894
19,500	35,788	4,686.9,942 + 46¢ for each $1 in excess of 19,500
35,788	..	12,179.4,742 + 60¢ for each $1 in excess of 35,788

The income tax rates for 1982-83 are a combination of the 1981-82 rates and a new scale that applied notionally from 1st November, 1982. Under the new scale the tax-free threshold was increased from Aus.$4,195 to Aus.$4,595, the standard rate of tax was reduced from 32 per cent to 30 per cent and the top of the standard rate step i.e. the point above which a taxpayer commences to pay 46 per cent of each additional dollar of income in tax was increased from Aus.$17,894 to Aus.$19,500. The maximum marginal rate of 60 per cent continued to apply to incomes above Aus.$35,788. In addition, from that date the dependent spouse rebate was increased from

Aus.$830 to Aus.$1,030 per year where there are dependent (including student) children. The same levels of rebate apply for a housekeeper or daughter-housekeeper where there are dependent children. The sole-parent rebate was also raised from Aus.$580 to Aus.$780 per year. The rates of tax applying for the 1982 (1982-83) year are an average of one-third of the 1981-82 scale and two-thirds of the scale applying notionally from 1st November, 1982. The maximum rebate for 1982-83 in respect of spouse, daughter-housekeeper, housekeeper, for taxpayers with dependent children is Aus.$963 and that for sole parent is Aus.$713.

As from 17th August, 1982, the tax-free threshold was withdrawn from non-resident taxpayers, other than those in receipt of Australian social security and repatriation pensions which are taxable in Australia and those who came to Australia on or before that date for a short working visit or who had made firm arrangements for such a visit by that date. A proportionate threshold of Aus.$585 applies to non-resident individual taxpayers for the 1982-83 income year.

A rebate was introduced for taxpayers in receipt of an Australian social security or repatriation pension which is subject to Australian income tax. The maximum rebate is Aus.$250 in a full year reducing by 12.5 cents for each Aus.$1 of taxable income in excess of Aus.$5,429. For 1982-83 the rebate is Aus.$167 with the result that for taxable incomes up to Aus.$5,006 no tax is payable for the 1982-83 income year.

A rebate of 30.67 per cent is allowable for the 1982-83 income year in respect of home loan interest payments made on or after 1st July, 1982 in connection with the purchase, construction or extension by a home-owner of a sole or principal residence in Australia. There are two schemes available and in a year of income a person will receive the benefit of the scheme which results in the greater rebate.

i) In the first scheme which applies to most home buyers the rebate is available on interest attributable to such part of the interest rate as exceeds 10 per cent per annum calculated on a reducing balance basis in respect of the first Aus.$60,000 of loans on a dwelling. The Government has announced that this scheme will not apply after the 1982-83 income year.

ii) The second scheme applies only to first-home buyers during the first five years of home ownership and the amount of the rebate available on all interest payments is subject to specified ceilings. This scheme will continue for low-income first-home buyers who enter the scheme on or before 30th September, 1983.

A rebate of 30.67 per cent is allowable for 1982-83 to resident individual shareholders on up to Aus.$1,000 of dividends included in taxable income and received from resident public or private companies or from non-resident companies the shares in which are listed on an Australian stock exchange.

Rebates for health insurance and concessional expenditure (which continued to apply to such expenses in excess of Aus.$1,590) were reduced from 32 per cent to 30.67 per cent.

AUSTRIA(1)

1. INCOME TAX

a) Tax Unit

Each person is taxed separately.

b) Tax Allowances and Tax Credits

Basic: Lump sum deduction for special expenses (available to all employees) A.Sch.3,276. Work-related expenses: a lump sum deduction of A.Sch.4,914 is given. Tax credits are available as follows: general tax credit of A.Sch.4,800; wage earner's tax credit of A.Sch.3,500; sole earner's tax credit of A.Sch.3,200; tax credit for retired persons A.Sch.2,000(2).

Marriage: A "sole-earner's" credit is given when a spouse either has no income or his/her income does not exceed A.Sch.10,000.

Children: A former tax credit of A.Sch.4,200 has been replaced by increased family allowance since 1978.

c) Schedule

The rates of tax are:

Up to A.Sch.50,000 tax at 21 per cent
Next A.Sch.50,000 tax at 27 per cent
Next A.Sch.50,000 tax at 33 per cent
Next A.Sch.50,000 tax at 39 per cent
Next A.Sch.50,000 tax at 45 per cent
Next A.Sch.50,000 tax at 50 per cent
Next A.Sch.200,000 tax at 55 per cent
Next A.Sch.500,000 tax at 58 per cent
Next A.Sch.500,000 tax at 60 per cent
   Remaining income tax at 62 per cent

---

1. APW gross earnings A.Sch.186,060.
2. Please refer to calculation of tax-free income and tax exemption for bonuses.

2. SOCIAL SECURITY CONTRIBUTIONS

a) Rate and Ceiling

	Ceilings		Rates	
	Regular wage	Christmas and leave bonus	Employee %	Employer %
Health insurance	A.Sch.18,000	A.Sch.36,000	3.15	3.15
Unemployment insurance	A.Sch.18,000	A.Sch.18,000	1.50	1.50
Pension insurance +additionals	A.Sch.21,600	A.Sch.43,200	9.75	11.35
Accident insurance	A.Sch.21,600	A.Sch.43,200	-	1.50
Contribution to the labour chamber	A.Sch.18,000	-	0.50	-
Contribution for residential aids	A.Sch.18,000	-	-	0.40
Contribution for the promotion for residential building	A.Sch.18,000	-	0.50	0.50
Contribution to secure continued wage payments	A.Sch.21,600	A.Sch.43,200	-	3.20
Addition to secure wage payments in the case of bankruptcy	A.Sch.18,000	A.Sch.18,000	-	0.50

d) Distinction by Marital Status or Sex

There is no differentiation between men and women, or between single and married persons.

3. CASH TRANSFERS

a) Amount for Marriage

No recurrent payments.

b) Amount for Children

A family allowance is granted for each child; it amounts at present to A.Sch.12,000 for each child and is increased up to A.Sch.14,400 from the beginning of the calendar year in which the child became ten years' old.

4. EFFECT ON TAX AND CASH TRANSFERS WHEN THE WIFE WORKS

a) On Husband's Allowances and Transfers

The sole-earner's credit is not given when a spouse's income exceeds A.Sch.10,000.

b) Special Treatment for Wife

None.

5. MAIN CHANGES SINCE 1982

None.

CANADA(1)

1. INCOME TAX

a) Tax Unit

Under the present system, the tax is levied on individuals separately; however, in cases where the income of a spouse (wife) is below $3,660 she reports her income on the return of the other spouse (husband). The husband receives a tax allowance in respect of his wife (maximum $3,110) which is reduced dollar for dollar by the amount of income accruing to the wife in excess of $550.

b) Tax Allowances and Tax Credits

Note: The personal exemptions (the basic allowance plus the allowance for a dependent spouse and dependent children) and the tax brackets of the personal income tax are indexed to offset the effects of inflation.

Basic: (Allowable to all taxpayers) $3,560. In addition to the basic personal exemption of $3,560, all taxpayers have the option of a $100 standard deduction in respect of medical expenses and charitable contributions, or they may claim:

a) actual medical expenses less 3 per cent of net income plus:
b) actual charitable contributions up to 20 per cent of net income.

Marriage: A taxpayer receives an allowance of $3,110 in respect of a dependent spouse, which is reduced in value depending on the amount of income accruing to the spouse [see 1(a) above].

Children: A taxpayer is allowed an exemption of $670 for each dependent child under the age of 18 whose income is less than $2,320. If the child's income is more than $2,320 but less than $3,660, the exemption is reduced by one-half of the child's income above $2,320.

For dependent children aged 18 and over, but under 21, the exemption is $1,220. The exemption is reduced by the amount of the dependent child's income over $2,440. Full-time students and infirm children over the age of 21 also qualify for the above deduction.

A refundable child tax credit was instituted beginning in 1978. For 1982, each family is eligible for a refundable tax credit of $343 per child under age 18 reduced by 5 per cent of family income in excess of $26,330.

---

1. In 1982, an Average Production Worker (APW) earned $22,067. All tax parameters refer to the 1982 taxation year.

Child-Care: A deduction is allowed in respect of children under the age of 14. The amount of the deduction is limited to the lesser of:

    i) the expenses incurred for the care of a child (maximum $30 per week per child for lodging at school or camp);
    ii) two-thirds of the taxpayer's earned income;
    iii) $1,000 for each child under age 14 to a maximum of $4,000.

The deduction is normally taken by the child's mother, but may be claimed by the child's father if he is a widower, or divorced or separated, or if the mother is infirm.

The average child care expense claimed per child was about $700 for the spouse earning the average production wage in 1980, the latest year for which complete data are available. About 34 per cent of claimants in this income range claimed the maximum $1,000 per child. However, this amount has not been used in the calculations of tax liability for the APW because less than 8 per cent of the tax filers take advantage of the deduction.

Work-related expense reliefs: Employees are entitled to an income deduction of 3 per cent of their annual wages with a maximum of $500 in the computation of their taxable income.

c) Schedule

Federal income tax rates before tax reductions range from 6 per cent on taxable income of $1,112 to 34 per cent on taxable income in excess of $53,376. There are 10 income tax brackets. These income tax brackets are indexed each year to offset inflationary increases in income. The table of tax rates is given below.

1982 FEDERAL INCOME TAX RATES
BASIC FEDERAL TAX

Taxable Income	Tax		
1,112 OR LESS	0 + 6%		0
1,112	67 + 16% on next		1,112
2,224	245 + 17% on next		2,224
4,448	623 + 18% on next		2,224
6,672	1,023 + 19% on next		4,448
11,120	1,868 + 20% on next		4,448
15,568	2,758 + 23% on next		4,448
20,016	3,781 + 25% on next		11,120
31,136	6,561 + 30% on next		22,240
53,376	13,233 + 34% on the rest		

General Federal Tax Reduction: The federal government provides a $200 non-refundable credit from federal tax payable. In the case of a married couple, each spouse qualifies for the $200 tax credit. Any unused portion of the credit can be transferred to the other spouse.

d) Local Income Taxes

In all provinces except one (Quebec), the provincial income tax is calculated as a percentage of basic federal tax [which is calculated before the general tax reduction - see (c) above]. The province of Quebec levies a separate income tax. The provincial tax rate is set by each province, and the rates applicable for 1981 are given in the table below.

1982 RATES OF PROVINCIAL INCOME TAX
(Percentage of basic federal tax)

Newfoundland	59.0%
Prince Edward Island	52.5%
Nova Scotia	56.5%
New Brunswick	55.5%
Ontario	48.0%
Manitoba	54.0%
Saskatchewan	51.0%
Alberta	38.5%
British Columbia	44.0%

Various provinces provide tax relief to low-income earners in the form of tax credits and some provinces levy surtaxes which primarily affect high income earners. The calculations for the APW study assume a provincial tax rate of 47 per cent which is a weighted average of the Canadian provincial rate.

2. SOCIAL SECURITY CONTRIBUTIONS

a) Rate and Ceiling

i) Old Age: Canada Pension Plan (CPP)

Generally, all employees are eligible for coverage under the Canada Pension Plan (Quebec Pension Plan in the province of Quebec). All employees are required to contribute to the Canada Pension at the rate of 1.8 per cent of income subject to contributions to a maximum of $268.20. Income subject to contributions is earnings (wages and salaries) less a $1,600 basic exemption. The maximum contribution of $268.20 is reached at an earnings level $14,900 [i.e. (16,500 - 1,600) x .018 = 268.20]. Employers are required to contribute to the Canada Pension Plan on behalf of their employees an amount equal to their employees' contributions. Thus, employers also contribute at the rate of 1.8 per cent of earnings (less the $1,600 earnings exemption) to a maximum of $268.20.

Self-employed persons are also required to contribute to the Canada Pension Plan. As there are no employer contributions for such persons, self-employed people are required to contribute 3.6 per cent of earnings up to a maximum of $536.40. As for employees, the maximum contribution of $536.40 is reached at an annual earnings level of $16,500. All contributions to the CPP or QPP are deductible from income subject to tax.

ii) Sickness

There is no national sickness benefit plan administered by the federal government, however, all provinces have provincially-administered health care insurance plans. Under certain circumstances, unemployment insurance benefits may be claimed in cases of illness.

iii) Work Injury

There is no national work injury benefit plan administered by the federal government. Each province, however, has a provincial workman's compensation plan which pays benefits to workers (or their families in case or death) for work-related illness or injury. These plans are funded entirely by employer contributions. The employer contribution rates, which vary by industry and by province, are related to industry experience of work-related illness and injury.

iv) Unemployment: Unemployment Insurance Commission

In general, all employees are eligible for unemployment insurance. For 1982, employees are required to contribute at the rate of 1.65 per cent of insurable earnings. Insurable earnings are earnings (wages and salaries) up to a maximum of $350 per week. The maximum employee contribution is $5.78 per week or $330.30 per year. The general employer contribution is 1.4 times the employee contribution, that is, 2.31 per cent of insurable earnings. Employers are rated on the basis of their previous lay-off experience and their premiums are adjusted accordingly. In addition, premiums are adjusted for employers who provide sick pay or health insurance plans superior to those provided under the UIC. All Unemployment Insurance Contributions are deductible from income subject to tax.

b) Distinction by Marital Status and Sex

Social security contributions are levied on individuals and the rates do not vary on the basis of marital status or sex.

3. CASH TRANSFERS

a) Amount for Marriage

None.

b) Amount for Children

Cash transfers in the form of family allowances are made at the rate of $26.91 per month for each child under the age of 18. This cash transfer, however, is taxable.

4. EFFECTS ON TAX AND CASH TRANSFERS WHEN THE WIFE WORKS

a) On Husband's Allowance and Transfers

If the wife's income is greater than $3,660, both husband and wife must file as separate individuals. If the wife's income is less than $3,660, the marital allowance of $3,110 is reduced by the excess of the wife's income over $550.

b) Special Treatment for Wife

A working mother may deduct child care expenses [see 1(b) above] incurred to permit her to work.

5. MAIN CHANGES SINCE 1982

Beginning with the 1982 taxation year, the Canadian tax system has been substantially modified. A number of tax preferences which were part of the tax base of the system were reduced or eliminated. At the same time, tax rates were lowered for higher-income taxpayers. The bracket limits and exemptions are still indexed. These amounts were increased by 12.2 per cent in 1982.

DENMARK(1)

1. INCOME TAX

a) Tax Unit

Spouses are taxed individually as regards earned income.

b) Tax Allowance and Tax Credits

In the assessment of income tax each person individually liable to tax is allowed a personal tax deduction. This allowance is deducted from the assessed income taxes.

The amount which forms the basis for calculations of the tax deduction is fixed at D.Kr.17,400 in 1982. For single pensioners the amount is D.Kr.34,800 and for married pensioners the deduction is fixed at D.Kr.19,000.

When a wife has no separate income, two personal tax deductions are allowed from the husband's assessed income taxes.

If a wife earns income which is taxed separately, her personal deduction is allowed from her assessed income taxes. Thus, the husband is allowed only his own personal deduction from his income taxes. If the income of either spouse is too small to make full use of the personal deduction, the balance is deducted from the income taxes of the other spouse.

The personal allowance mentioned provides for separate reductions of income tax to the State, social security contributions and local income taxes (including income taxes to the Church). The allowance is converted for reduction of income tax to the State by the lowest marginal rate of tax (14.4 per cent). Reductions of social security contributions and local income taxes are calculated by use of tax rates applicable to the taxpayer in question dependent on his age and permanent address.

Examples:

Taxpayer under 67 years of age (not being a pensioner) and with permanent address in the municipality with lowest total Local Income Tax rate.

---

1. In 1982 the Average Production Worker earned D.Kr.141,200.

| | Personal tax deduction | |
	D.Kr.	D.Kr.
Income Tax to the State	(17,400 x 14.4%)	2,506
Social Security Contributions	(17,400 x 4.5%)	783
Local Income Taxes	(17,400 x 18.3%)	3,184
Total	(17,400 x 37.2%)	6,473

Taxpayer aged 67 and upwards (a single pensioner) and with permanent
address in the municipality with highest total Local Income Tax rate.

| | Personal tax deduction | |
	D.Kr.	D.Kr.
Income Tax to the State	(34,800 x 14.4%)	5,011
Social Security Contributions	(34,800 x 4.5%)	1,566
Local Income Taxes	(34,800 x 29.4%)	10,231
Total	(34,800 x 48.3%)	16,808

Basic: One personal deduction and a wage-earner's standard deduction
of D.Kr.3,200 are granted. As to the personal deduction see the information given above.

c) Central Government Tax Schedule 1981

Taxable income   D.Kr.   0 to D.Kr. 95,200 at 14.4 per cent
Taxable income   D.Kr .95,500 to D.Kr. 164,100 at 28.8 per cent
Taxable income over D.Kr.161,400 at 39.6 per cent

d) Local Income Tax

Local income tax is payable by individuals to the authority of the
municipality in which they are a resident.

The basis of assessment is the ordinary taxable income as assessed for
national income tax purposes. County, municipal and church tax in total
is levied at a flat rate which varies between 18.3 - 29.4 per cent in
1982. The average rate for the whole country is calculated as being
25.6 per cent.

The average rate is calculated on the basis of reports from the muni-
cipalities. The rate is calculated by taking the estimated revenues from
local income taxes as a percentage of the estimated "schedule income" (i.e.
taxable income minus personal tax deductions) for the whole country.

2. SOCIAL SECURITY CONTRIBUTIONS

a) Rate and Ceiling

Employees

For all taxpayers, contributions to the National Pension Scheme and the Sickness Payments Scheme amount to a 4.5 per cent flat rate calculated on the basis of taxable income(1). That sort of contribution is collected with central government income tax. The employee's contribution to the Unemployment Insurance Premium typically amounts to D.Kr.950.

Employers

The employers' contribution to the unemployment insurance is D.Kr.633 per head. However, one employee is free.

b) Distinction by Marital Status or Sex:

None.

3. CASH TRANSFERS

a) Amount for Marriage:

None.

b) Amount for Children:

The following cash transfers are given:

In the case of single persons with dependants:

- D.Kr.5,795 for the first child;
- D.Kr.3,283 for each subsequent child;

In the case of married persons with dependants

- D.Kr.2,184 per child.

(When "social income" exceeds D.Kr.156,000 no cash transfer is scaled down. The so-called social income is a modified concept of taxable income.)

---

1. A personal tax deduction is allowed. See pp. 1-2, and p. 5.

4. EFFECT ON TAX AND CASH TRANSFERS WHEN THE WIFE WORKS

a) <u>On Husband's Allowances and Transfers</u>:

The husband loses half of his personal deduction (i.e. that granted in respect of the non-working wife)(2).

b) <u>Special Treatment for Wife</u>:

None.

5. MAIN CHANGES SINCE 1982

a) <u>The Standard Deduction for Wage and Salary Earners</u>

The amount was raised from D.Kr.2,000 in 1981 to D.Kr.3,200 in 1982.

b) <u>Social Security Contributions Which are Collected with Central Government Income Tax</u>

In 1981 the contributions consisted of a <u>National Pension Scheme</u> contribution (1.2 per cent of taxable income), a <u>Special National Pension Scheme</u> contribution (2 per cent of taxable income) and a <u>Sickness Benefit Scheme</u> contribution (1 per cent of taxable income).

According to the rules in 1981 all persons with full tax liability were obliged to pay contributions to the National Pension Scheme and the Sickness Benefit Scheme. Liability for payment to the Special National Pension Scheme ceased at the end of the calendar year in which the taxpayer reached 67. So in 1981, the total social security contributions collected with central government income tax amounted to 4.2 per cent of taxable income for taxpayers under 67 and 2.2 per cent for taxpayers over 67.

According to the rules for 1982 there was no liability for payment to the Special National Pension Scheme. However, the contribution to the National Pension Scheme was raised from 2.2 per cent to 3.5 per cent of taxable income. Those changes implied that for all taxpayers the total social security contributions collected with central government income tax in 1982 amounted to 4.5 per cent of taxable income. So for taxpayers under 67 the total amount was raised from 4.2 per cent to 4.5 per cent and for taxpayers over 67 the total amount was raised from 2.2 per cent to 4.5 per cent.

---

2. See Section 1 (b) above.

6. EMPLOYEE'S SECURITY CONTRIBUTIONS

	Men only		Men and women
	Single	Married	Single
	D.Kr.	D.Kr.	D.Kr.
Health insurance premium	-	-	-
Unemployment insurance premium	950	950	950
Old-age pension contributions: 3.5 per cent of taxable income exceeding D.Kr.17,400 for single persons and D.Kr.34,800 for married couples	4,221	3,612	4,046
Sickness Benefit contributions: 1 per cent of taxable income exceeding D.Kr.17,400 for single persons and D.Kr.34,800 for married couples	1,377	1,032	1,156
TOTAL	6,377	5,594	6,152

7. ADDITIONAL INCOME TAX DUE TO POLITICAL SUBDIVISIONS

County, municipal and church tax, average rate for the whole country 25.6 per cent of taxable income exceeding:

> D.Kr.17,400 for single persons
> D.Kr.34,800 for married couples

8. CASH TRANSFER PAYMENTS FROM GENERAL GOVERNMENT

Subsidy to children, D.Kr.2,184 for each child

ESPAGNE

1. IMPOT SUR LE REVENU DES PERSONNES PHYSIQUES (année 1981)

1.   L'impôt sur le revenu des personnes physiques est un tribut de caractère direct et de nature personnelle qui frappe la totalité des rendements nets en plus des accroissements de patrimoine de l'unité contribuante, en fonction de son montant et des circonstances personnelles et familières qui se sont produites.

L'unité contribuante, dont ses rendements s'accroissent aux effets de l'impôt, est composée du ménage et des enfants mineurs.

2. Le tarif

L'assiette de l'impôt devient grevée selon un tarif progressif dont ses taux fiscaux varient entre 15 % pour les assiettes inférieures jusqu'à 200.000 pesetas et 65,09 % pour les assiettes supérieures à 10.600.000 pesetas. La cote totale ne pourra pas excéder cependant 40 % de l'assiette.

Les contribuables, dont les rendements sont inférieurs à 300.000 pesetas, ne sont pas dispensés de l'obligation de faire la déclaration.

3. Déductions

On peut déduire de la cote résultante moyennant l'application du tarif, entre autres, les montants suivants :

- Avec caractère général   15.000 pesetas

- Pour ménage   12.500   "

- Pour chaque enfant   10.000   "

- Pour des frais nécessaires sans qu'aucune
  justification ne soit requise   10.000   "

Il y a d'autres déductions au sujet des circonstances familières, d'âge ou de maladie et pour investissements ; spécialement lorsque les deux conjoints perçoivent des rendements du travail, la déduction générale de 15.000 pesetas augmente quand un taux multiple est appliqué.

D'autre part, on attache la considération d'investissement, et le droit au crédit fiscal de 15 % aux montants qui sont destinés à l'acquisition d'un logis propre.

2. CONTRIBUTIONS DE LA SECURITE SOCIALE

a) Taux et plafond

Le revenu assujetti à la Contribution de la Sécurité Sociale est divisé en deux parties, comme suit :

   i) La première concerne le revenu grevé selon un tableau révisé périodiquement ;
   ii) La deuxième comprend n'importe quel revenu restant (salaires supplémentaires).

Les taux sont les suivants :

   i) En ce qui concerne (i) au-dessus d'un taux de 40 % s'applique : 35 % est payé par les employeurs et 5,5 % par les employés.
   ii) En ce qui concerne (ii) au-dessus un taux de 14 % s'applique : 12 % est payé par les employeurs et 2 % par les employés.

b) Distinction à cause du statut marital ou du sexe

Aucune

3. TRANSFERTS AU COMPTANT

a) Montant pour ménage

Un montant de 375 pts. est donné par mois pour l'épouse.

b) Montant pour enfants

Un montant additionnel de 300 pts. par mois est donné pour chaque enfant à charge.

4. EFFET SUR TRANSFERTS FISCAUX ET AU COMPTANT LORSQUE L'EPOUSE TRAVAILLE

a) Sur les subventions et transferts du mari

Aucun

b) Traitement spécial pour l'épouse

Aucun.

FINLAND(1)

1. INCOME TAX

a) Tax Unit

Spouses are taxed separately for earned income.

b) Tax Allowances and Tax Credits

Basic: The basic deduction against earned income is 25 per cent of earned income up to a maximum amount of Fmk.9,000. The spouse with the lower income may deduct 20 per cent of earned income up to the maximum amount of Fmk.4,100 if there are dependant children. This maximum amount is Fmk.5,100 if the age of the child is at most 7 years.

Marriage: The spouse with more income may deduct Fmk.4,500 if the other spouse has no income. However, if the other spouse has income the deduction is reduced by 25 per cent of the income of the spouse with lesser income.

Children: A tax credit is granted for each dependant child. The amount of the tax credit is:

for the first child	Fmk. 650
for the second child	Fmk. 750
for the third child	Fmk. 900
for the fourth child and subsequent children	Fmk.1,200

c) Schedule

State income tax.

Taxable income Fmk	Tax at the Lower Limit of the Bracket Fmk	Rate of Excess over the Lower Limit
11,500 - 15,500	10	6
15,500 - 19,100	250	13
19,100 - 23,600	718	19
23,600 - 29,100	1,573	23
29,100 - 38,100	2,838	28
38,100 - 55,000	5,358	29
55,000 - 74,000	10,259	33

---

1. In 1982, the Average Production Worker earned Fmk.58,229.

Taxable Income Fmk	Tax at the Lower Limit of the Bracket Fmk	Rate of Excess over the Lower Limit
74,000 - 114,000	16,529	38
114,000 - 191,000	31,729	45
191,000 - 342,000	66,379	50
342,000 -	141,879	51

d) Local Income Tax

Municipal tax is levied at flat rates. Every resident individual with an income of less than Fmk.6,800 is, however, entitled to a deduction before the rate of tax is applied to his income. In 1982, the tax rate varied between 14 and 18.5 per cent, the average rate being approximately 15.9 per cent.

Municipal taxes are not deductible against central government taxes.

Child deduction: Fmk.1,250 for each dependent child. Work-related expenses are deductible, as in the State income taxation.

2. SOCIAL SECURITY CONTRIBUTIONS

a) Rate and Ceiling

In 1982, the rate of the social security contribution paid by an employee was 2.82 per cent, 1.82 percentage point of which was for the National Pension Scheme and 1 percentage point for the National Sickness Scheme. The tax base for the social security contribution is the net taxable income in municipal income taxation. (This taxable income is lower for families with children due to the child deduction.)

b) Distinction by Marital Status or Sex

The rates do not differ, but the tax to be paid by a one-parent family is lower because he or she is entitled to the sole-parent's deduction.

3. CASH TRANSFERS

a) Amount for Marriage

None.

b) Amount for Children

The central government pays the following allowances:

for the first child   Fmk.1,482
for the second child   Fmk.1,714
for the third child   Fmk.1,996
for the fourth and subsequent
children   Fmk.2,546

If the child is less than three years old, an additional child allowance of Fmk.853 is paid. The child allowance is paid to the mother, except where the father is the head of a one-parent family.

4. EFFECT ON TAX AND CASH TRANSFERS WHEN THE WIFE WORKS

a) On Husband's Allowances and Transfers

Husband gradually loses allowance as wife's income increases.

b) Special Treatment for Wife

None.

5. MAIN CHANGES SINCE 1982

Inflation adjustment for tax schedule and allowances has been made.

FRANCE (1)

1. L'IMPOT SUR LE REVENU

a) Unité d'imposition

L'unité d'imposition est le revenu commun de la famille ; mais les enfants n'y sont compris que s'ils sont à la charge des parents. Les autres personnes (grand-mère, etc.) sont prises en compte sous certaines conditions. Contrairement aux conjoints qui sont toujours imposés ensemble, les enfants et les autres membres de la famille ont la faculté de choisir l'imposition séparée.

b) Abattements et crédits d'impôt

Abattement à la base : les abattements accordés sont les suivants :

- 10 % du montant net des salaires et traitements, cette déduction forfaitaire étant au minimum de F 1 800 et plafonnée à F 50 900 ;
- des déductions supplémentaires sont accordées à certaines professions ;
- un abattement supplémentaire égal à 20 % du salaire, déduction faite des cotisations de sécurité sociale et du (ou des) abattement(s) sus-mentionné(s), s'il n'excède pas 460 000 (abattement maximum égal à F 92 000).

Personnes mariées : le système du "quotient familial" permet de tenir compte de la situation et des charges de famille du contribuable. Il consiste à diviser le revenu total net en un certain nombre de parts d'après un schéma pré-établi qui correspond à la situation du contribuable et au nombre de personnes à sa charge : l'impôt total dû est égal au montant de l'impôt correspondant à une part multiplié par le nombre total de parts (une part pour le mari, une part pour la femme, une demi-part pour chaque enfant et autre personne à charge) ; les contribuables ayant 3 enfants et plus bénéficient d'une demi-part supplémentaire. Cependant l'avantage en impôt résultant du fonctionnement du quotient familial est plafonné à F 7 500 par demi-part excédant 1 part pour un contribuable célibataire, divorcé ou veuf, ou deux parts pour un contribuable marié.

Enfants à charge : l'abattement résulte normalement du jeu du quotient familial. Toutefois, un régime spécial est prévu pour le cas des enfants de plus de 18 ans poursuivant leurs études ou accomplissant leur service militaire. En outre, les chefs de famille sans conjoint peuvent déduire les dépenses occasionnées par la garde de leurs enfants âgés de moins de 4 ans, à concurrence de F 3 000 par enfant et à condition que leur revenu net soit inférieur à F 145 880.

---

1. en 1982, l'ouvrier moyen gagnait F 68 735.

c) <u>Barème</u> (pour une part) applicable en 1982 sur les revenus de 1981

Fraction du revenu inférieure à			F	11 230	: 0 %
Fraction du revenu comprise entre	F 11 230	et	F	11 740	: 5 %
	F 11 740	et	F	13 930	: 10 %
	F 13 930	et	F	22 030	: 15 %
	F 22 030	et	F	28 320	: 20 %
	F 28 320	et	F	35 590	: 25 %
	F 35 950	et	F	43 060	: 30 %
	F 43 060	et	F	49 680	: 35 %
	F 49 680	et	F	82 790	: 40 %
	F 82 790	et	F	113 860	: 45 %
	F 113 860	et	F	134 680	: 50 %
	F 134 680	et	F	153 200	: 55 %
Au-delà de			F	153 200	: 60 %

- si le montant d'impôt excède F 25 000, une majoration de 10 % est appliquée à la fraction de l'impôt excédant F 15 000 ;
- pour les personnes seules dont l'impôt est inférieur à F 2 600 (une part) ou F 800 (1,5 part) il est accordé un crédit d'impôt égal à la différence entre l'impôt calculé et ces montants ;
- en outre l'impôt n'est pas mis en recouvrement si son montant est inférieur à F 240.

2. COTISATIONS DE SECURITE SOCIALE

a) <u>Taux et plafond</u>

Les pourcentages appliqués au revenu brut sont les suivants :

- <u>maladie, maternité, invalidité</u> :

  5,50 % sur le gain total

- <u>assurance vieillesse de base</u> :

  4,70 % à concurrence d'un plafond de F 60 120

- <u>Chômage</u>

  0,84 % jusqu'à F 240 480 de rémunération

- <u>assurance vieillesse complémentaire</u> :

  minimum 1,76 % jusqu'à F 180 360 de rémunération pour les salariés non cadres. Pour les salariés cadres, 1,76 % jusqu'à F 60 120 et 2,06 % minimum pour la fraction du salaire comprise entre F 60 120 et F 240 480

b) <u>Distinction selon la situation de famille ou le sexe</u>

  Aucune.

3. PRESTATIONS EN ESPECES

a) <u>Pour les personnes mariées</u>

Aucune.

b) <u>Pour enfants à charge</u>

Les montants accordés sont les suivants (en moyenne annuelle) :

- 2 818,26 F pour le deuxième enfant ;
- 5 089,56 F pour le troisième enfant ;
- 4 566,60 F pour le quatrième enfant ;
- 4 321,50 F à partir du cinquième enfant.

Une majoration de F 1 102,80 est accordée pour chaque enfant (à l'exception de l'aîné dans les familles qui n'ont que deux enfants) âgé de 10 à 15 ans et une majoration de F 1.960,56 pour tout enfant de plus de 15 ans.

En outre, les familles de condition modeste reçoivent une allocation de rentrée scolaire à 218,65 F pour chaque enfant âgé de 6 à 16 ans. De plus une majoration exceptionnelle de 150 F pour chaque enfant a été versée au mois de février 1980.

Les ménages ou personnes qui remplissent les conditions d'ouverture du droit aux prestations familiales et qui assument la charge soit d'au moins un enfant de moins de trois ans, soit d'au moins trois enfants, bénéficient sous condition de ressources d'un complément familial.

Plafond de ressources : (revenu net imposable 1979) = F 35 780 majoré de 25 % par enfant à charge. Pour déterminer les ressources à comparer au plafond, il est pratiqué sur le revenu un abattement pour double activité professionnelle ou personne seule de F 7 860.

Montant mensuel du complément familial = F 395 au 1er janvier 1980 ; F 455 au 1er juillet 1980 soit pour l'ensemble de l'année F 5 100.

Une allocation différentielle est versée aux ménages ou personnes qui bien que remplissant les conditions d'attribution disposent de ressources dépassant le plafond d'une somme inférieure à douze fois le montant mensuel du complément familial en vigueur au 1er juillet de l'année de référence.

4. INCIDENCE DE L'ACTIVITE PROFESSIONNELLE DE LA FEMME MARIEE SUR LES ABATTEMENTS FISCAUX ET LES PRESTATIONS EN ESPECES

Aucune.

5. PRINCIPALES MODIFICATIONS INTERVENUES DEPUIS 1982

Aucune.

GERMANY

(1982)

1. INCOME TAX

a) Tax Unit

Spouses are normally assessed jointly. They have, however, the option of being separately assessed. The income of dependent children is not assessable with that of the parents.

b) Tax Allowances and Tax Credits

The following are the main allowances for employees that are automatically taken into account in the tax deducted by the employer:

1) DM.1,644 (or DM.3,288 where both spouses are gainfully employed) for work-related expenses and selective tax relief for employees.
2) DM.270 (DM.540 where spouses are assessed jointly) for other expenses.
3) 18 per cent of gross earnings (up to specific ceilings) for social security contributions and other expenses incurred in provision for the future.

On application to the tax office, the following expenses may also be taken into account in the deduction of wages tax or on assessment (wages tax annual adjustment):

- Work-related expenses in excess of the lump-sum allowance;
- Expenses incurred in provision for the future (up to specific ceilings) which are not covered by the relevant lump-sum allowance.

Marriage

In the case of joint assessment, specific allowances are doubled (see above). Income tax according to the schedule is computed by the income splitting method.

c) Schedule

The German tax schedule is a formula-based schedule.

The calculations are based on a rounded amount of taxable income. If the taxable income cannot be divided by 54 it is rounded down to the next (full DM -) amount which can be divided by 54.

X is the rounded taxable income.
T is the income tax liability.

In addition the following definitions are used in the income tax liability formulas:

$$Y : = \frac{X - 18,000}{10,000};$$

$$Z : = \frac{X - 60,000}{10,000};$$

The income tax liability (amounts in Deutsche Mark) is calculated as follows:

a) Formula

    1) T =   0 for X   4212
    2) T =   0.22 X - 926 for 4213   X   18,000
    3) T =   [(3.05 Y - 73.76)·Y+695]·Y+2,200 ·Y+3.034
              for 18.001   X   59999
    4) T =   [(0.09·Z-5.45)·Z+88.13]·Z+5040   ·Z+20 018
              for 60,000   X   129 999
    5) T =   0.56 X - 14837 for 130 000   X

These formulas are used directly to calculate the income tax of single persons.

The income tax liability for spouses who are assessed jointly is computed as follows:

The formula income tax is calculated with respect to one-half of the joint taxable income. The resulting amount is doubled to arrive at the income tax liability of the spouses (splitting method).

Social Security Contributions

In the case of dependent employees, contributions to old age, unemployment and sickness insurance amount on average to 34 per cent of gross earnings (up to specific ceilings). As a rule, employee and employer each pay half (i.e. 17 per cent) of these contributions. If the employee's earnings are below a certain level, these contributions are paid by the employer alone. Contributions to accident insurance are paid by the employer.

a) Old Age, Invalidity, Survivors' Pensions

The contributions amount to 18 per cent of gross earnings, not exceeding 18 per cent of the insurable ceiling. In 1982, this was set at DM.56,400.
Employee's contribution: 9 per cent of gross earnings, or not more than 9 per cent of the insurable ceiling.

b) Unemployment

Contributions: 4 per cent of gross earnings.
Insurable ceiling: DM.56,400.
Employee's contribution: 2 per cent of gross earnings, or not more than 2 per cent of the insurable ceiling.

c) Sickness

Contributions: on average 12 per cent of gross earnings.
Insurable ceiling: DM.42,300.
Employee's contribution: on average 6 per cent of gross earnings,
or not more than 6 per cent of the insurable ceiling.

d) Accident

The purpose of accident insurance is to provide employees and their
survivors with social protection against the consequences of acci-
dents at work.
The contributions to accident insurance are paid by the employer
alone. They are based on employees' earnings and on the danger
classes in which individual enterprises are classified according to
the incidence of risk.

3. CASH TRANSFERS

a) Marriage

None.

b) Amount for Children

DM. 600 a year for the first child;
DM.1,200 a year for the second child;
DM.2,640 a year for the third child;
DM.2,880 a year for the fourth and subsequent child.

4. EFFECT ON TAX AND CASH TRANSFERS WHEN THE WIFE WORKS

a) On Husband's Allowances and Transfers

None.

b) Special Treatment for Wife

None.

5. MAIN CHANGES SINCE 1982

None.

GREECE(1)
(1981)

1. INCOME TAX

a) Tax Unit

The income of spouses is generally assessed separately.

b) Tax Allowances and Tax Credits

Basic: A personal allowance of Drs.20,000 is given.

Marriage: An additional deduction of Drs.20,000 is allowed for the wife.

Children: The following allowances are given for children:

Drs.15,000 for the first child
Drs.15,000 for the second child
Drs.25,000 for the third child
Drs.35,000 for the fourth and subsequent children

Our figures exclude sickness and unemployment compensations. Normal overtime bonuses are included in the basic series. Benefits in Kind are excluded.

The APW is not assumed to live in any particular locality.

2. SOCIAL SECURITY CONTRIBUTIONS

a) Rate and Ceiling

Employees pay 9 per cent of gross wage, up to a ceiling of Drs.50,025 per month.

Employers pay 17 per cent of gross wage, up to a ceiling of Drs.50,025 per month.

b) Distinction by Marital Status and Sex

None.

---

1. In 1982, the Average Production Worker earned Drs.469,196.

79

3. CASH TRANSFERS

a) Amount for Marriage

The husband receives an amount equal to 10 per cent of his earnings as a marriage allowance.

b) Amount for Children

The husband gets an amount equal to 10 per cent of his earnings for each child.

4. EFFECT ON TAX AND CASH TRANSFERS WHEN THE WIFE WORKS

a) On Husband's Allowances and Transfers

None.

b) Special Treatment for Wife

If the income of the husband is insufficient to absorb the dependant's allowance, the balance is deducted from the wife's income.

5. MAIN CHANGES SINCE 1981

A major tax reform is underway.

ITALY(1)

1. INCOME TAX

a) Tax Unit

In April, 1977, joint taxation of husbands and wives was abolished and spouses are now entitled to separate assessment.

b) Tax Allowances and Tax Credits

Basic: There is no basic allowance. There is, however, a tax credit of L.36,000 given to all taxpayers, another which is given to all earners, and a credit for expenses.

Marriage: For 1982 a tax credit of L.180,000 is given; provided the spouse's income is less than L.1,350,000.

Children: A married person whose spouse has an income of less than L.1,350,000 is given a tax credit of L.36,000 for the first child, L.82,000 for the second child. If the spouse's income exceeds L.1,350,000, half the above amounts is given to each spouse.

Other members of the family: A tax credit of L.12,000 is granted for other dependants.

A dependant is defined as any person entitled to maintenance allowances (e.g. parents, mother and father-in-law) under civil law.

c) Scale

Until	3	million L.				10 per cent	
from	3	"	until	4	million L.	13	" "
"	4	"	"	5	"	16	" "
"	5	"	"	6	"	19	" "
"	6	"	"	7.5	"	22	" "
"	7.5	"	"	9	"	25	" "
"	9	"	"	11	"	27	" "
"	11	"	"	13	"	29	" "
"	13	"	"	15	"	31	" "
"	15	"	"	17	"	32	" "
"	17	"	"	19	"	33	" "
"	19	"	"	22	"	34	" "
"	22	"	"	25	"	35	" "
"	25	"	"	30	"	36	" "
"	30	"	"	35	"	38	" "

---

1. In 1982, the Average Production Worker earned L.11,447,520.

from	35	million L. until	40	million L.	40 per cent
"	40	"	"	50	"	42 " "
"	50	"	"	60	"	44 " "
"	60	"	"	80	"	46 " "
"	80	"	"	100	"	48 per cent
"	100	"	"	125	"	50 " "
"	125	"	"	150	"	52 " "
"	150	"	"	175	"	54 " "
"	175	"	"	200	"	56 " "
"	200	"	"	250	"	58 " "
"	250	"	"	300	"	60 " "
"	300	"	"	350	"	62 " "
"	350	"	"	400	"	64 " "
"	400	"	"	450	"	66 " "
"	450	"	"	500	"	68 " "
"	500	"	"	550	"	70 " "
from	550	"	"			72 " "

2. SOCIAL SECURITY CONTRIBUTIONS

a) Rate and Ceiling

The rate was 7.45 per cent.

b) Distinction by Marital Status or Sex

None.

3. CASH TRANSFERS

a) Amount for Marriage

A taxable transfer of L.233,580 is given for each child.

4. EFFECT ON TAX AND CASH TRANSFERS WHEN THE WIFE WORKS

a) On Husband's Allowances and Transfers

Tax credits are unaffected when the wife works but the cash transfer given for marriage is lost. When the wife's income exceeds L.1,350,000 the husband loses the credit of L.180,000 given for a dependent wife. As was the case for 1975, the cash transfer for marriage is lost.

b) Special Treatment for Wife

The working wife is given the same deductions as the husband.

5. MAIN CHANGES SINCE 1982

None.

1. INCOME TAX

a) <u>Tax Unit</u>

Tax is levied on the combined income of both spouses. Either spouse may, however, opt for separate assessment, in which case the tax payable by both spouses must be the same as would be payable under joint taxation. A further option allows either spouse to opt for assessment as single persons in which case they are treated as separate units.

b) <u>Tax Allowances and Tax Credits</u>

<u>Basic</u>: The single person's allowance is £1,450 per year.

<u>Marriage</u>: The married person's allowance is £2,900 per year (i.e. twice the basic allowance of £1,450).

<u>Employee Allowance</u>: £600.

<u>Special Pay-Related Social Insurance Allowance</u>: £312

<u>Children</u>: The child allowance is £100 per year.

c) <u>Schedule</u>

Band of taxable income		Rate per cent
Single/Widow(er)	Married Couple	
First £1,000	£2,000	25
Next £3,000	£6,000	35
Next £2,000	£4,000	45
Next £2,000	£4,000	55
Balance		60

2. SOCIAL SECURITY CONTRIBUTION

a) <u>Rate and Ceiling</u>

From 6th April, 1981 employees' social security contributions were payable at a rate of 4.75 per cent of earnings subject to a ceiling of £8,500. The employer's rate of contribution was 10.05 per cent of earnings subject to the same ceiling.

_____

1. In 1982, the Average Production Worker earned an estimated £7,652.

From 6th April, 1982 the employees' rate was raised to 7.5 per cent. 6.5 per cent was subject to a ceiling of £9,500 while the remaining 1 per cent, known as the "youth employment levy", applied to all earnings. The employers' rate of contribution was raised to 11.61 per cent subject to the £9,500 ceiling.

b) Distinction by Marital Status or Sex

None.

3. CASH TRANSFERS

a) Amount for Marriage

None.

b) Amount for Children

Social Welfare children's allowances are payable in respect of all children under 16 years (or under 18 years, if undergoing full-time education).

The amounts payable are:

Effective date	Monthly Rate	
	First child	Second and each subsequent child
	£	£
January, 1982	6.00	9.00
April, 1982	11.25	11.25

4. EFFECT ON TAX AND CASH TRANSFERS WHEN THE WIFE WORKS

a) On Husband's Allowance and Transfers

Where joint assessment applies the husband's position is not affected. However where separate or single assessment applies the result will be a transfer of allowances from husband to wife. Generally it is to the advantage of married taxpayers to opt for joint assessment which allows any balance of the unused allowances of one spouse to accrue to the benefit of the other. However, in certain limited circumstances, where one spouse qualifies for exemption, single assessment may be more beneficial.

Transfers are generally payable to the wife.

b) Special Treatment for Wife

The working wife is not subject to any special treatment. As an employee she is entitled to the employee allowance. Otherwise her income is effectively treated for tax purposes as an extra increment on her husband's income. The allowances and rate bands for married persons are of course double those for single persons.

5. MAIN CHANGES SINCE 1982

The 1983 budget further extended the general exemption limits which were first introduced in 1980. The exemption limit for single, widowed and married persons who opt to be assessed as single persons was increased from £2,200 to £2,400. The limit for a married man where the couple opts for joint assessment was increased from £4,400 to £4,800. A new rate of 65 per cent was introduced to apply to taxable income over £10,000 in the case of single and widowed persons and double that amount in the case of married taxpayers. The pay related social insurance allowance, temporarily introduced in 1982/83 to give relief to persons paying the higher rates of social insurance, was reduced from £312 to £286 for the purpose of funding a new social welfare family income supplement for lower-paid families.

In 1982/83 a temporary 1 per cent levy called the "youth employment levy", earmarked for combating youth unemployment, was imposed on all personal income. Though collected through the social security collection system it was not subject to the ceiling applying thereto. This levy has continued in 1983/84 and a further 1 per cent levy known as the "income levy" has now been introduced. While applied in the same manner as the youth employment levy, the income levy is not earmarked for any specific purpose.

JAPAN

1. INCOME TAX

a) Tax Unit

In the case of earned income, the individuals of the family are taxed separately.

In the case of unearned income, to prevent any reduction in tax burden by arbitrarily distributing income from assets among family members in one household, such distributed income is aggregated for tax purposes on certain conditions.

b) Tax Allowances and Tax Credits

Basic Exemption: A resident taxpayer is entitled to an exemption of Yen.290,000.

Exemption for Spouse: A spouse who lives with a taxpayer and does not gain income is entitled to an exemption of Yen.290,000.

Exemption for Dependents: Each dependent is entitled to an exemption of Yen.290,000.

Deduction for Employment Income: In the case of employment income, a certain percentage of receipts is deducted for tax purposes from total receipts.

c) Schedule

The tax schedule is as follows.

Taxable income brackets (Yen. per year)	Marginal rates %
- 600,000	10
600,000 - 1,200,000	12
1,200,000 - 1,800,000	14
1,800,000 - 2,400,000	16
2,400,000 - 3,000,000	18
3,000,000 - 4,000,000	21
4,000,000 - 5,000,000	24
5,000,000 - 6,000,000	27
6,000,000 - 7,000,000	30
7,000,000 - 8,000,000	34
8,000,000 - 10,000,000	38
10,000,000 - 12,000,000	42
12,000,000 - 15,000,000	46

Table continues on next page

```
15,000,000 - 20,000,000                              50
20,000,000 - 30,000,000                              55
30,000,000 - 40,000,000                              60
40,000,000 - 60,000,000                              65
60,000,000 - 80,000,000                              70
80,000,000 -                                         75
```

2. SOCIAL SECURITY CONTRIBUTIONS

a) Rate and Ceiling

There are five kinds of social insurance: medical insurance, public pensions, employment insurance, workmen's accident compensation insurance, and child allowance programmes.

The contributions are shared between employee and employer as follows:

1. Employee

i) Health Insurance

   - 4.25 per cent of standard remuneration (male and female)
   - Special contribution; 0.3 per cent of bonuses (male and female)

ii) Employee's Pension Insurance

   - Male   5.3 per cent of standard remuneration
   - Female 4.6 per cent of standard remuneration

iii) Employment Insurance

   0.55 per cent of total remuneration (male and female)

iv) Workmen's Accident Compensation Insurance

None.

v) Child Allowance

None.

"Standard remuneration" includes compensation for overtime, but does not include bonuses. The ceilings of remuneration are Yen.470,000 per month for Health Insurance and Yen.410,000 per month for Employee's Pension Insurance.

2. Employer

i) Health Insurance

   - 4.25 per cent of standard remuneration (male and female)
   - Special contribution; 0.5 per cent of bonuses (male and female)

ii) Employment Insurance

   - Male   5.3 per cent of standard remuneration
   - Female 4.6 per cent of standard remuneration

iii) Employment Insurance

    0.9 per cent of total remuneration (male and female)

iv) Workmen's Accident Compensation Insurance

    0.5 - 12.9 per cent of total remuneration (male and female)

v) Child Allowance

    0.09 per cent of standard remuneration

b) Distinction by Marital Status of Sex

    See above under 2 (a).

3. CASH TRANSFERS

a) Amount for Marriage

    None.

b) Amount for Children

    A cash transfer is given for the third and subsequent children provided they are below 18 years of age.

4. EFFECT ON TAX AND CASH TRANSFERS WHEN THE WIFE WORKS

a) On Husband's Allowances and Transfers

    None.

b) Special Treatment for Wife

    In certain cases, the allowance given for a spouse is withdrawn.

5. MAIN CHANGES SINCE 1982

None.

LUXEMBOURG (1)

1. IMPOT SUR LE REVENU

a) Unité d'imposition

Les époux sont imposés collectivement sur leur revenu. Les revenus des enfants mineurs sont à mettre en compte dans le calcul du revenu imposable des époux. Ne tombent cependant pas sous l'imposition collective les revenus que les enfants tirent d'une occupation salariée.

b) Abattements et crédits d'impôt

Il est déduit à titre de frais d'obtention un minimum forfaitaire de 21 000 F pour les revenus nets provenant d'une occupation salariée. Les contribuables salariés bénéficient en plus d'un abattement de revenu imposable de 18 000 F. Il est déduit au titre des dépenses spéciales du total des revenus nets un minimum forfaitaire de 15 000 F.

Personnes mariées et enfants à charge : aucun abattement ou crédit d'impôt ne sont prévus ; les dispositions tarifaires prennent en considération l'état civil du contribuable et le nombre des enfants à charge.

c) Barème

L'impôt sur le revenu est déterminé conformément au tarif de base suivant :

0 %	pour la tranche de revenu inférieure à					F 99 600
12 %	pour la tranche de revenu comprise entre	F 99 600	et	F 110 400
14 %	"	"	F 110 400	et	F 129 000
16 %	"	"	F 129 000	et	F 147 600
18 %	"	"	F 147 600	et	F 166 800
20 %	"	"	F 166 800	et	F 189 000
22 %	"	"	F 189 000	et	F 211 800
24 %	"	"	F 211 800	et	F 234 000
26 %	"	"	F 234 000	et	F 273 000
28 %	"	"	F 273 000	et	F 312 000
30 %	"	"	F 312 000	et	F 351 000
33 %	"	"	F 351 000	et	F 390 000
36 %	"	"	F 390 000	et	F 429 000
39 %	"	"	F 429 000	et	F 468 600
42 %	"	"	F 468 600	et	F 510 000
45 %	"	"	F 510 000	et	F 552 000
48 %	"	"	F 552 000	et	F 594 000

---

1. En 1982, l'ouvrier moyen gagnait F 558 200.

90

50 %	"	"	F 594 000	et	F 663 600
52 %	"	"	F 663 600	et	F 733 200
54 %	"	"	F 733 200	et	F 865 800
56 %	"	"	F 865 800	et	F 1 068 000

57 % pour la tranche de revenu dépassant F 1 068 000

L'impôt à charge des contribuables célibataires est déterminé par l'application du tarif de base ; toutefois, lorsque le revenu ne dépasse pas F 246 000 il est réduit du cinquième de son complément à F 246 000. L'impôt à charge des contribuables mariés correspond au double de la cote qui correspond par l'application du tarif à la moitié du revenu. L'impôt des contribuables ayant des enfants à charge est déterminé de la façon suivante :

1. Dans les hypothèses où le nombre des charges d'enfants ne dépasse pas trois unités et où le revenu n'excède pas F 579 000, le revenu est divisé en parts suivant le nombre des charges d'enfants. Le revenu correspondant à une part est taxé par application du tarif ; la cotisation ainsi obtenue, multipliée par le nombre de parts, donne l'impôt dû. Le nombre de parts à prendre en considération pour la division du revenu est fixé comme suit :
   2,6 pour une charge d'enfant,
   3,4 pour deux charges d'enfants,
   4,6 pour trois charges d'enfants.

Dans toutes les autres hypothèses, l'impôt est égal à l'impôt dû pour un même revenu par un contribuabble de la classe II diminué d'une bonification pour enfants.

a) Si le revenu ne dépasse pas 1 269 000 F, la bonification s'élève à :

   1 % du revenu plus 15 716,40 F pour une charge d'enfant,
   2 % du revenu plus 30 667,20 F pour deux charges d'enfants,
   3 % du revenu plus 46 458 F pour trois charges d'enfants,
   4 % du revenu plus 56 592 F pour quatre charges d'enfants.

Pour les charges d'enfants en sus de la 4ème, la bonification est égale à celle prévue pour 4 charges d'enfants augmentée de 1 % du revenu plus 10 134 F pour chaque charge supplémentaire.

b) Si le revenu est compris entre 1 269 000 F et 1 654 200 F la bonification est de :

   28 406,40 F pour une charge d'enfant,
   56 047,20 F pour deux charges d'enfants,
   84 528   F pour trois charges d'enfants,
   107 352 F pour quatre charges d'enfants.

Pour les charges d'enfants en sus de la 4ème, la bonification est égale à celle prévue pour 4 charges d'enfants augmentée de 22 824 F pour chaque charge supplémentaire.

c) Si le revenu dépasse 1 654 200 F, la bonification prévue à l'alinéa b, est à diminuer pour les charges d'enfants en sus de la première de 2 % de la différence entre le revenu et 1 654 200 F et de 1 548 F à partir d'un revenu de 1 731 600 F.

	Taux	Plafond

Assurance-vieillesse   janvier - décembre : 8 %   Aucun plafond
   et invalidité   cotisable

Assurance-maladie   4 %   Le maximum cotisable est
                                                        égal à 4 fois le salaire
                                                        social minimum pour un
                                                        travailleur non qualifié
                                                        de 18 ans.

                         Maximum cotisable :
                         janvier   : 86 664 F
                         février à
                         août   : 88 828 F
                         septembre à
                         novembre   : 91 048 F
                         décembre   : 93 324 F

Aucune distinction n'est faite selon la famille ou le sexe.

3. ALLOCATIONS EN ESPECES

a) Pour les personnes mariées

   Aucune

b) Pour enfants à charge

   Le montant des allocations familiales ordinaires accordées pour deux enfants a été de 45 648 F.

4. INCIDENCES DE L'ACTIVITE PROFESSIONNELLE DE LA FEMME MARIEE SUR LES ABATTEMENTS FISCAUX ET LES PRESTATIONS EN ESPECES

a) Sur les abattements et prestations accordés au mari

   Aucune.

b) Situation spéciale de la femme mariée (salariée)

   Les forfaits pour frais d'obtention et dépenses spéciales ainsi que l'abattement compensatoire sont doublés dans le chef des époux salariés imposables collectivement.

5. PRINCIPALES MODIFICATIONS INTERVENUES DEPUIS 1982

Le forfait pour dépenses spéciales est porté de 15 000 francs à 18 000 francs et le tarif de base ainsi que les montants tarifaires concernant les modérations d'impôt pour charge(s) d'enfant(s) ont été actualisés en raison de la variation du coût de la vie.

Le nouveau tarif de base est le suivant :

0 % pour la tranche de revenu inférieure à				F	108 000
12 % pour la tranche de revenu comprise entre	F 108 000	et	F	120 000	
14 % " "	F 120 000	et	F	140 400	
16 % " "	F 140 400	et	F	160 800	
18 % " "	F 160 800	et	F	180 600	
20 % " "	F 180 600	et	F	205 200	
22 % " "	F 205 200	et	F	229 800	
24 % " "	F 229 800	et	F	253 800	
26 % " "	F 253 800	et	F	297 000	
28 % " "	F 297 000	et	F	339 000	
30 % " "	F 339 000	et	F	381 600	
33 % " "	F 381 600	et	F	424 200	
36 % " "	F 424 200	et	F	466 200	
39 % " "	F 466 200	et	F	508 800	
42 % " "	F 508 800	et	F	554 400	
45 % " "	F 554 400	et	F	600 000	
48 % " "	F 600 000	et	F	645 600	
50 % " "	F 645 600	et	F	721 200	
52 % " "	F 721 200	et	F	796 800	
54 % " "	F 796 800	et	F	940 800	
56 % " "	F 940 800	et	F 1 160 400	
57 % pour la tranche de revenu dépassant			F 1 160 400		

NETHERLANDS

1. INCOME TAX

a) Tax Unit

Earned income of husband and wife is taxed separately.

b) Tax Allowances and Tax Credits

Basic: A single taxpayer up to 35 years of age gets an allowance of
DFL.7,010. A single taxpayer of 35 years and over and all divorced taxpayers get an allowance of DFL.9,423,=. An allowance of DFL.12,078 per
year is given to a married man, and to a married woman with own earned income an allowance of DFL.2,241 is given. An income related expense allowance equal to 4 per cent of earned income is given (minimum DFL.200,= maximum DFL.800,=).

Also a minimum allowance of DFL.200,= is given for the cost of travel-
ling to work. Employee's social security contributions are deductible with
the exception of the health insurance contribution.

c) Schedule

The 1982 rate schedule is as follows:

Zero	-	9,269	17 per cent
9,269	-	15,702	26 3/4 per cent
15,702	-	28,498	32 3/4 per cent
28,498	-	39,753	40 3/4 per cent
39,753	-	57,545	50 3/4 per cent
57,545	-	80,385	59 3/4 per cent
80,385	-	105,921	64 3/4 per cent
105,921	-	137,345	67 3/4 per cent
137,345	-	200,194	70 3/4 per cent
200,194 and over			72 3/4 per cent

2. SOCIAL SECURITY CONTRIBUTIONS

d) Rate and Ceiling

The employee pays social security contributions as follows:

- 4.05 per cent sickness and unemployment premium (ceiling DFL.66,033).
- Invalidity premium: 11.9 per cent (ceiling DFL.66,033; franchise DFL.22,968).
- 4.55 per cent health insurance premium if income is below DFL.43,450 (ceiling DFL.37,062).
- 12.5 per cent general old age premium and widows' and orphans' premium (ceiling DFL.57,050).

b) Distinction by Marital Status or Sex

None.

3. CASH TRANSFERS

a) Amount for Marriage

None.

b) Amount for Children

The following amounts apply to children under 18 years of age:

One child	DFL. 1,150
Two children	DFL. 3,016
Three children	DFL. 4,880
Four children	DFL. 7,136
Five children	DFL. 9,390
Six children	DFL.11,876
Seven children	DFL.14,364
Eight children	DFL.17,104
Subsequent children	DFL. 2,740

4. EFFECT ON TAX AND CASH TRANSFERS WHEN THE WIFE WORKS

a) On Husband's Allowances and Transfers

When a married woman becomes employed this can affect the net income of the husband, because the general old age premiums and the widows' and orphans' premiums are computed on the couple's joint income. If the total of these premiums exceeds the maximum of DFL.7,131,= the excess is paid back to the husband.

b) Special Treatment for Wife

The working wife gets a tax allowance of DFL.2,421,=.

5. MAIN CHANGES SINCE 1981

1. Inflation adjustment of tax allowances and brackets.

2. Increase of the tax rates, except the lowest, by 3/4 per cent.

3. Adjustment of ceilings for social security contributions and of cash transfers to children.

4. Changes of rates for social security contributions. Shift from employers' contributions to employees' contributions.

NEW ZEALAND

1. INCOME TAX

a) Tax Unit

Members of the family are taxed separately.

b) Tax Allowances and Tax Credits

Basic

A standard allowance of 2 per cent of salary and wages to a maximum of $52 or actual employment-related expenditure within defined limits.

"Principal Income Earner Rebate"

Rebate for principal income earner, single person or solo parent may claim the rebate provided:

- income was less than $14,600, and
- spouse's income, if any, is less than the principal income earner's.

Rebate is 2.75 cents for each complete dollar of income if total income is $5,672 or under, or

- if total income is between $5,672 and $12,000, rebate is $156
- if total income is between $12,000 and $14,600, rebate reduces by 6 cents for each complete dollar of income in excess of $12,000. No rebate if total income exceeds $14,600.

Marriage

Rebate for spouse of $78 provided his/her income does not exceed $520. Rebate is reduced by 10 cents for each dollar earned by spouse in excess of $520. Rebate ceases when spouse's earnings reach $1,300 per annum.

Children

No rebates to parents.

However, a rebate of $117 is allowable to a <u>child</u> who is under 15 years of age or under 18 years of age if still attending an educational institution and if the family benefit is payable in respect of the child.

<u>Note</u>: The rebate must be claimed by the child, <u>NOT</u> the parents or guardians.

"Family Rebate"

Allowable to the principal income earner (includes widows, widowers and solo parents) in a family with a child for whom the family benefit is payable.

Provided income was less than $19,160 or where spouse also has income, the combined total incomes of both taxpayer and spouse was less than $19,160. Rebate $702 if combined total income was $9,800 or less.

Rebate reduces 7.5 cents for each dollar of income in excess of $9,800. No claim where the combined total income exceeds $19,160.

Note: Where a taxpayer qualifies for both the Principal Income Earner and Family Rebate, only the greater of the two is claimable.

Young Family

Rebate of up to $234 per annum is allowed to the spouse with the higher income level, provided:

i) The family includes a child under 5 years of age during the income year for whom the family benefit is payable.
ii) The income level does not exceed $13,700 per annum.
iii) The rebate reduces by 6 cents for each dollar earned over $13,700 and ceases when the earnings reach $17,600.

Low Income Family

Rebate of up to $234 per annum is allowed to the spouse with the higher income level, provided:

i) The family includes a child for whom the family benefit is payable, i.e., no age limit, could be up to 18 years of age if attending an educational institution.
ii) The combined incomes of both spouses does not exceed $9,800 per annum.
iii) The rebate reduces by 6 cents for each dollar of the combined spouses' income earned in excess of $9,800 and ceases when the combined incomes reach $13,700.

c) Schedules

Rates of income tax - individuals: year ended 31st March, 1983 (period 1st April, 1982 to 31st March, 1983)

On so much of the income as -	The rate of Tax for every $ shall be - Cents
Does not exceed $5,500	17.25
Exceeds $5,500 but does not exceed $6,000	27.5
Exceeds $6,000 but does not exceed $12,600	33.0

	Cents
Exceeds $12,600 but does not exceed $17,600	39.5
Exceeds $17,600 but does not exceed $22,000	43.0
Exceeds $22,000 but does not exceed $24,000	45.5
Exceeds $24,000 but does not exceed $30,000	52.55
Excceds $30,000 but does not exceed $38,000	58.05
Exceeds $38,000	63.0

2. SOCIAL SECURITY CONTRIBUTIONS

No contributions.

3. CASH TRANSFERS

a) Amount for Marriage

None.

b) Amount for Children

Family benefit (exempt from taxation) is payable to the mother in the normal family situation, to the father only if solo parent. Each child under 16 years - $6.00 per week. Each student child 16 to 18 years - $6.00 per week up to the eighteenth birthday or end of school year, whichever is the latter.

4. EFFECT ON TAX AND CASH TRANSFERS WHEN SPOUSE WORKS

On spouses' allowances and transfers:

i) Rebate for spouse is reduced by 10 cents for each dollar earned by spouse over $520. Rebate ceases when spouse's earnings exceed $1,300 per annum.
ii) Family Rebate refer same under I.B.
iii) Low income family refer same under I.B.
iv) Principal Income Earner Rebate refer under same I.B.
v) Family benefit is paid to the mother irrespective of the level of her earnings and does not affect any of the rebates.

5. MAIN CHANGES SINCE 1982 (year ended 31st March, 1982)

- Introduction of Principal Income Earner Rebate
- Introduction of Family Rebate
- Reduction in level of Young Family Rebate
- Reduction in level of Low Income Family Rebate
- Alteration to marginal tax rates to include reductions.

NORWAY

1. INCOME TAX

a) Tax Unit

Married couples are jointly taxed under the class 2 schedule. They can, however, opt to be taxed individually (class 1) if this is more favourable. Children less than 17 years old are generally taxed with their parents, but may be taxed individually. All other income earners are taxed individually.

b) Central Government Income Tax

Tax allowances

Basic: In the assessment of income tax and the health insurance contributions each taxpayer gets a minimum deduction equal to 10 per cent of gross income, with a minimum of NKr.1,600 and maximum of Nkr.3,100.

The taxpayer also has a "computation deduction" from income equal to 4 per cent of income, with a minimum of Nkr.400 and maximum of Nkr.700.

Children: The tax reduction for children less than 17 years old are Nkr.1,000 and the reduction are Nkr.1,400 for children between the ages of 17 and 20 years who do not have an income of their own. The tax deduction goes on the total amount of taxes and social security contributions and is spread proportionately to the tax liability on each kind of taxes.

Special tax reduction for 1982

The income tax liability that is the result from the central government rate schedule, the local government income tax, and the employee's social security contributions shall be reduced by 0.8 per cent of gross income up to Nkr.110,000, by 0.6 per cent of the part of the income between Nkr.110,000 and Nkr.165,000, and by 0.3 per cent of the part of the income between Nkr.165,000 and Nkr.248,000. This tax deduction will only affect the central government tax revenue. The individual taxpayer will, however, get a reduction in his total taxes finally paid even if this reduction is bigger than the tax liability resulting from the central government rate schedule.

Married couples: Married couples have a deduction from their own taxable income amounting to:

- 25 per cent of income, maximum Nkr.600, when they have children between the ages of 14 and 20 years.
- 40 per cent of income, maximum Nkr.3,500, when they have one child younger than 14 years.
- 50 per cent of income, maximum Nkr.4,500, when they have two or more children younger than 14 years.

If the family can documentate child-care expenses, the couple will get a reduction up to the double at the above-mentioned limits. These deductions also apply for families with children where the wife or husband is single. The deduction applies to the spouse who has the largest income.

Rate Schedule

	Class 1	Class 2
0% up to Nkr	38,000 -	68,000 -
6%	38,000 - 72,000	68,000 - 94,000
11%	72,000 - 86,000	94,000 - 108,000
17%	86,000 - 98,000	108,000 - 120,000
23%	98,000 - 111,000	120,000 - 133,000
28%	111,000 - 133,000	133,000 - 155,000
33%	133,000 - 166,000	155,000 - 188,000
38%	166,000 - 250,000	188,000 - 272,000
43%	250,000 -	272,000

c) Local Government Income Tax

The municipal, country, etc. income tax rate is 23 per cent. The deductions available under these taxes are:

Nkr. 9,500 in class 1
Nkr.19,000 in class 2

d) Limitation on Total Tax Payable

The total tax payable on income and property may not exceed 80 per cent of taxable income under the central government income tax.

2. SOCIAL SECURITY CONTRIBUTIONS

e) Contributions to the National Insurance Scheme

Employers' contribution is 8.6, 12.6, 14.6 and 16.8 per cent of wage income depending on where the employees have their residence. The average is about 16.3 per cent. The pension-part: Employees' contributions on wage income is 5.7 per cent. Employees' contributions on other income is 10.6 per cent.

The Health Insurance Part: Employees' contribution is 4.4 per cent of the taxable income on the municipal tax assessment.

3. CASH TRANSFERS

The following transfers are given:

- Nkr.3,252 for the first child

- Nkr.4,008 for the second child
- Nkr.5,028 for the third child
- Nkr.5,412 for the fourth child
- Nkr.6,204 for the fifth and subsequent child.

4. EFFECT ON TAX OF CASH TRANSFERS WHEN THE WIFE WORKS

a) <u>On Husband's Allowances and Transfers</u>

   None.

b) <u>Special Treatment for the Wife</u>

   See Section 1 (b) above.

5. MAIN CHANGES SINCE 1982

   1. Increase in cash transfers for children with NKr.492 to Nkr.600 per child.

   2. Increase in the local government income tax deductions with Nkr.1,000 for class 1 and Nkr.2,000 for class 2.

   3. Increase in employees' pension-part contribution from 5.3 per cent to 5.7 per cent for wage income and from 10.2 per cent to 10.6 per cent for other income.

   4. Increase in special reduction in income tax with 3 per cent.

PORTUGAL (1)

1. IMPOT SUR LE REVENU

Le système d'imposition sur le revenu est constitué par un ensemble d'impôts réels cédulaires, qui font la distinction des revenus d'après leur source et auxquels s'ajoute un impôt de superposition - appelé Impôt Complémentaire qui, dans le cas des personnes physiques vise à personnaliser dans une certaine mesure, l'imposition du revenu.

En ce qui concerne l'étude de l'ouvrier moyen on considère seulement l'impôt professionnel et l'impôt complémentaire, étant donné que les gains moyens sont constitués exclusivement par revenus du travail.

a) Unité d'imposition

Les impôts cédulaires sont perçus sur les revenus des conjoints séparément, alors que l'impôt global (complémentaire) (2) est perçu sur le revenu commun de la famille. Depuis 1980, mais étant applicables aux revenus de l'année 1979 et suivantes, il existe deux barèmes pour l'impôt complémentaire : l'un pour les contribuables non mariés et séparés judiciairement de personnes et de biens, l'autre pour les contribuables mariés ou non séparés judiciairement de personnes et de biens.

b) Abattements et crédits d'impôt

Il n'est accordé de déductions qu'au titre de l'impôt global (complémentaire).

Au revenu brut il est accordé un abattement équivalent au montant des impôts cédulaires et des cotisations pour la sécurité sociale et le Fonds de Chômage, déjà payés.

Abattement de base : il est accordé un abattement de Esc. 100 000 au profit du contribuable non marié, veuf ou séparé judiciairement de personnes et de biens,

ou

Un abattement de Esc. 150.000 au profit des deux conjoints non séparés judiciairement de personnes et de biens.

---

1. En 1982, l'ouvrier moyen gagnait Esc.234 720 (estimation).
2. L'impôt complémentaire sera payé au cours de l'année suivant celle à laquelle le revenu se rapporte.

Un abattement supplémentaire de 30 % sur le revenu salarial brut du contribuable et du conjoint (lorsque la femme travaille) à concurrence de Esc. 100 000 (Esc. 50 000 pour chacun).

Enfants à charge : les abattements accordés au titre d'enfants à charge dépendent de l'âge des enfants ; ils s'établissent comme suit : Pour chaque enfant, adopté ou beau-enfant, mineur, non émancipé ou incapable pour le travail et de prévoir à sa propre subsistance, n'étant pas un assujetti de l'impôt complémentaire :

Jusqu'à 11 ans .... Esc. 20 000
Plus de 11 ans .... Esc. 30 000

Lorsque le nombre d'enfants est égal ou supérieur à 5 la déduction minimale sera Esc. 150 000.

Pour chaque enfant, adopté ou beau-enfant, majeur jusqu'à 24 ans, qui, au cours de l'année à laquelle l'impôt regard, ait étudié, inscrit dans un établissement d'enseignement moyen ou supérieur, obtenant approbation scolaire...Esc. 30 000.

c) Barème

Impôt professionnel

Le barème de l'impôt professionnel est applicable aux revenus bruts des deux conjoints séparément donc sans aucun abattement de base. Les revenus jusqu'à Esc. 160 000 sont exemptés.

Les taux du barème se rangent de 2 %, pour les revenus au-dessus de Esc. 160 000, jusqu'à 22 %, taux applicable aux revenus supérieurs à Esc. 1 350 000.

Impôt complémentaire

L'impôt complémentaire a deux barèmes :

i) Le barème applicable aux contribuables non mariés ou séparés judiciairement de personnes et de biens varie de 4,8 % (taux commun) pour un revenu imposable inférieur à Esc. 180 000 à 80 %, taux applicable à la part du revenu imposable supérieure à Esc. 2 280 000.

ii) Le barème applicable aux contribuables mariés et non séparés judiciairement de personnes et de biens, commence au taux (commun) de 4 % pour un revenu imposable inférieur à Esc. 180 000 jusqu'à 70 %, taux applicable à la partie du revenu imposable supérieure à Esc. 2 280 000.

Les taux susmentionnés concernent les revenus pour l'année 1982.

2. COTISATIONS DE SECURITE SOCIALE

a) Taux et plafond

Les taux de cotisations de sécurité sociale frappent les salaires bruts sans aucun plafond.

En règle générale, le taux des cotisations des employé(e)s est de 8 % (depuis décembre 1979).

Les cotisations des employé(e)s pour le Fonds de Chômage sont fixées à 2,5 % depuis le 1er janvier 1976.

Les cotisations de sécurité sociale des employeurs ont un taux de 21 % (depuis septembre 1981).

   i) moitié du salaire d'un
      ouvrier moyen .... Esc. 117.360 x 21 % = Esc. 24.646
  ii) salaire d'un ouvrier moyen . Esc. 234.720 x 21 % = Esc. 49.292
 iii) salaire double de celui d'un
      ouvrier moyen .... Esc. 469 440 x 21 % = Esc. 98.582

b) Distinction selon la situation de famille ou de sexe

Le taux des cotisations est indépendant de la situation de famille du travailleur.

3. PRESTATIONS EN ESPECES (depuis juin 1981)

a) Pour les personnes mariées

Esc. 4.800 pour chaque conjoint lors du mariage (pourvu qu'ils soient couverts par la Prévoyance Sociale).

b) Pour enfants à charge

Esc. 5.500 accordés à la famille lors de la naissance de chaque enfant, et Esc. 1 080 d'allocation d'allaitement, pendant dix mois, pourvu que l'un des parents soit couvert par la Prévoyance sociale.

Une allocation de Esc. 450 par mois et par enfant accordée à la famille. Cette allocation est de Esc. 520 pour le troisième enfant et de Esc. 600 pour le quatrième enfant et suivants.

Il y a aussi un régime spécial d'allocation familiale pour les enfants handicapés.

Les prestations en espèces ci-mentionnés, alinéas a) et b), ne sont pas imposables.

4. INCIDENCE DE L'ACTIVITE PROFESSIONNELLE DE LA FEMME MARIEE SUR LES ABATTEMENTS FISCAUX ET LES PRESTATIONS EN ESPECES

a) Sur les abattements et prestations accordés au mari

Aucune incidence (la déclaration de l'impôt complémentaire est établi par les deux conjoints).

b) <u>Situation spéciale de la femme mariée</u> (salariée)

La femme mariée qui travaille bénéficie d'une déduction de 30 % sur son revenu salarial brut à concurrence de Esc. 50.000 (v.g. ci-dessus n° 1 alinéa b abattements de base).

5. PRINCIPALES MODIFICATIONS INTERVENUES DEPUIS 1982

Aucune.

SUISSE 1982[1]

Les impôts cantonaux et communaux sur le revenu sont très importants par rapport à l'impôt fédéral pour la défense nationale (IDN). On a retenu ici, à titre d'exemple du régime d'imposition des 26 cantons, celui qui est pratiqué dans le canton de Zurich. L'impôt local (canton et commune) sur le revenu n'est pas déductible pour le calcul de l'impôt fédéral sur le revenu.

1. IMPOT SUR LE REVENU

a) Unité d'imposition

Le mari est habituellement imposable sur son revenu propre, ainsi que sur celui de sa femme et sur les revenus non salariaux de ses enfants mineurs vivant au foyer (les revenus salariaux de ces derniers sont imposés séparément ou sont parfois exonérés d'impôt, à Zurich par exemple).

b) Abattement et crédits d'impôt

Abattement à la base = Dépenses professionnelles

L'abattement à la base varie à Zurich en fonction de la catégorie professionnelle (de 1 200 à 1 800 FS). Toutefois, au titre de l'impôt pour la défense nationale, (d'impôt fédéral direct) l'abattement à la base est de 1 200 FS.

Déductions personnelles

En ce qui concerne l'impôt cantonal et communal, dans le canton de Zurich, les personnes célibataires bénéficient d'une déduction de 3 000 FS, les personnes mariées de 6 000 FS.

Pour le calcul de l'IDN, seules les personnes mariées bénéficient d'une déuction de 2 500 FS. En outre, les contribuables mariés peuvent déduire, en plus de la déduction personnelle de 2 500 FS sur le revenu imposable :

    20 % des premiers 200 FS du montant de l'impôt
    10 % des 200 FS suivants
     5 % des 200 FS suivants.

---

(1) En 1982, l'ouvrier moyen gagnait 40 100 francs suisses.

Enfants à charge

Le régime d'imposition des revenus appliqué dans le canton de Zurich prévoit un abattement de 1 800 francs suisses pour chaque enfant âgé de moins de 19 ans ou pour chaque enfant en apprentissage ou poursuivant des études. L'impôt pour la défense nationale comporte le même abattement (1 200 FS) pour chaque enfant âgé de moins de 18 ans, ainsi que pour tout enfant en apprentissage ou poursuivant des études.

c) Barème

IMPOT POUR LA DEFENSE NATIONALE

Revenu imposable (1) FS	Montant de base FS	% de la partie qui dépasse	FS
jusqu'à 9 699	-	-	-
9 700 à 22 000	22,-	1,1	9 700
22 000 à 38 500	157,30	3,3	22 000
38 500 à 55 000	701,80	6,6	38 500
55 000 à 71 500	1 790,80	8,8	55 000
71 500 à 93 500	3 242,80	11,0	71 500
93 500 à 392 800	5 662,80	13,2	93 500
392 800	45 170,40	-	-
392 900 et plus	45 183,50	11,5	392 900

(1) Les fractions inférieures à 100 FS sont négligées.

IMPOT CANTONAL SUR LE REVENU (Zurich)

a) TAUX SIMPLES de l'impôt sur le revenu pour les personnes mariées, divorcées, veuves ou célibataires avec enfants vivant dans le ménage propre

Revenu imposable (2) FS	Montant de base FS	plus ...% de la partie qui dépasse	FS
jusqu'à 4 000	-	2	-
4 000 à 8 000	80	3	4 000
8 000 à 13 000	200	4	8 000
13 000 à 19 000	400	5	13 000
19 000 à 25 000	700	6	19 000
25 000 à 31 000	1 060	7	25 000
31 000 à 40 000	1 480	8	31 000
40 000 à 55 000	2 200	9	40 000
55 000 à 75 000	3 550	10	55 000
75 000 à 95 000	5 550	11	75 000
95 000 à 125 000	7 750	12	95 000
plus de 125 000	11 350	13	125 000

(2) Les fractions inférieures à 100 FS sont négligées.

b) TAUX SIMPLES de l'impôt sur le revenu pour les autres personnes
   (célibataires sans enfants)

Revenu imposable[3] FS	Montant de base FS	...% de la partie qui dépasse	plus FS
jusqu'à 3 000	-	2	-
3 000 à 6 000	60	3	3 000
6 000 à 10 000	150	4	6 000
10 000 à 15 000	310	5	10 000
15 000 à 20 000	560	6	15 000
20 000 à 25 000	860	7	20 000
25 000 à 31 000	1 210	8	25 000
31 000 à 43 000	1 690	9	31 000
43 000 à 59 000	2 770	10	43 000
59 000 à 75 000	4 370	11	59 000
75 000 à 125 000	6 130	12	75 000
Plus de 125 000	12 130	13	125 000

3) Les fractions inférieures à 100 FS sont négligées.

c) MULTIPLE ANNUEL   des taux légaux simples

- Canton de Zurich   120 %

- Commune de Zurich   133 %

- Impôt paroissial
  cath. rom.   13 %
  réform.   11 %

2. COTISATIONS DE SECURITE SOCIALE

a) Taux et plafond

Genre d'assurance	Taux en pour cent	
	Salariés	Employeurs
Assurance-vieillesse et invalidité	5 1)	5 1)
Assurance-chômage	0,15 2)	0,15 2)
Pension	5 3)	5 3)

1) Du revenu salarial brut.
2) Du revenu salarial brut, au maximum 70 FS (revenu annuel de
   46 700 FS).
3) En moyenne, du revenu salarial brut pour la cotisation aux caisses de
   retraite des entreprises.

b) Distinction selon la situation de famille ou le sexe

Aucune.

3. PRESTATIONS EN ESPECES

a) Pour les personnes mariées

Aucune.

b) Pour enfants à charge

Aucune prestation en espèces n'est versée directement par l'Etat, mais une allocation est versée et payée par l'employeur (canton de Zurich : minimum 70 FS par enfant et par mois) ; elle est considérée comme faisant partie du salaire du travailleur et imposée à ce titre.

4. INCIDENCE DE L'ACTIVITE PROFESSIONNELLE DE LA FEMME MARIEE SUR LES ABATTEMENTS FISCAUX ET LES PRESTATIONS EN ESPECES

a) Sur les abattements et prestations accordés au mari

Aucune.

b) Situation spéciale de la femme mariée

La femme mariée bénéficie d'une déduction (Déduction du revenu de l'activité de la femme mariée : 2 000 FS pour l'IDN - 3 000 FS à Zurich).

5. PRINCIPALES MODIFICATIONS INTERVENUES DEPUIS 1980

Aucune modification essentielle.

SWEDEN(1)

1. INCOME TAX

a) Tax Unit

Spouses are taxed separately.

b) Tax Allowances and Tax Credits

	Central government taxation	Local government taxation
	If a person had no work-related expenses or such expenses less than Sw.Kr.100 then it was possible to reduce income from employment with Sw.Kr.100	The same rule as for central government taxation
Basic	No basic deduction from assessed income	A basic deduction of Sw.Kr.7,500 from assessed income
Marriage	A maximum tax reduction of Sw.Kr.1,800 was possible if wife had no income	No married reliefs
Tax credit	None	None
Children	No relief	No relief

c) Schedules

The table refers to central government income tax for income year 1982.

Taxable income in Swedish kroner	Tax amount in Swedish kroner and %
- 6,900	0
6,900 - 27,600	0 + 2%
27,600 - 48,300	414 + 4%
48,300 - 55,200	1,242 + 9%
55,200 - 62,100	1,863 + 14%
62,100 - 69,000	2,829 + 23%
69,000 - 82,800	4,416 + 26%
82,800 - 89,700	8,004 + 29%
89,700 - 96,600	10,005 + 33%
96,600 - 103,500	12,282 + 38%

---

1. 1982 an Average Production Worker earned Sw.Kr.84,600.

Taxable income in Swedish kroner	Tax amount in Swedish kroner and %
103,500 - 110,400	14,904 + 44%
110,400 - 117,300	17,940 + 45%
117,300 - 138,000	21,045 + 48%
138,000 - 207,000	30,981 + 53%
207,000	67,551 + 58%

The average local income tax for income year 1982 was 29.74 per cent.

c) Local Income Tax

See above.

2. SOCIAL SECURITY CONTRIBUTIONS

Social security contributions are levied on employers only. Contributions for basic pension, supplementary pension and health insurance added up to 28.35 per cent of the total sum of wages and salaries paid in 1982.

3. CASH TRANSFERS

a) Amount for Marriage

None.

b) Amount for Children

Sw.Kr.3,000 for each child.

4. EFFECT ON TAX AND CASH TRANSFERS WHEN THE WIFE WORKS

a) On Husband's Allowances and Transfers

The tax reduction given for marriage varies when the wife works and no reduction is given when she earns more than Sw.Kr.6,000.

When both spouses are gainfully employed and they have children under 16 years of age then the one who has the lowest income may claim an earned income deduction of maximum Sw.Kr.2,000.

b) Special Treatment for Wife

Same as under (a) above.

5. MAIN CHANGES SINCE 1982

None.

UNITED KINGDOM(1)

1. INCOME TAX 1982/83

a) Tax Unit

Tax is levied on the joint income of the spouses, unless a couple elects to have the wife's earnings taxed separately. In that event, the husband is taxed on the remainder of the joint income, including any un-earned income of the wife. The income of other members of the family is taxed separately.

b) Tax Allowances and Tax Credits

Basic: A single person's allowance of £1,565 is granted.

Marriages: Under the United Kingdom legislation, the basic allowance and the marriage allowance given to a married couple together form one allowance which is £880 more than the single person's allowance.

Children: Apart from a few special cases there are no tax allowances for children.

c) Schedule

The tax schedule comprises six brackets. Details are shown below.

Slice of total income (after deductions)	Rate
£	%
0 - 12,800	30
12,800 - 15,100	40
15,100 - 19,100	45
19,100 - 25,300	50
25,300 - 31,500	55
over 31,500	60

The general principle of aggregation of the husband's and wife's income means that, with a system of progressively higher rates of tax on each suc-cessive slice of income, couples in the higher income bracket are - in spite of the married man's allowance taxed more highly on their earnings than two single people with the same income. That is why the couple may jointly elect to have the wife taxed on her earnings as if she were a single woman with no other income.

---

1. In 1982 an Average Production Worker earned £7,467.

a) Employee's Contribution

National Insurance Contributions are payable on the first £220 of gross weekly earnings by all employees earning £29.50 a week or more. The standard rate of contributions is 8.75 per cent, but a married woman may elect to pay at a reduced rate of 3.2 per cent. In this case she is insured under the Industrial Injuries Scheme only and will not receive benefits under the National Insurance Scheme, except insofar as she may be entitled to them by virtue of her husband's contributions.

Most widows are also liable to contribute at the reduced rate and elderly and retired people above a certain age are exempt.

b) Employer's Contribution

Employers' Contributions are payable at a rate of 10.2 per cent plus 3 1/2 per cent surcharge (reduced to 2 per cent in August 1982) on earnings of up to £220 a week on behalf of all employees earning £29.50 a week or more. This rate applies whether the employee pays contributions at the standard rate, the reduced rate, or not at all.

3. CASH TRANSFERS

a) Amount for Marriage

None.

b) Amount for Children

A tax-free benefit is given to a family with children under 16 (for a child continuing at school or apprenticed with low earnings). In April 1982 the weekly rate was £5.25 rising to £5.85 in November.

4. EFFECT ON TAX AND CASH TRANSFERS WHEN THE WIFE WORKS

a) On Husband's Allowances and Transfers

None.

b) Special Treatment for Wife

The wife received a tax allowance equivalent to the basic allowance.

5. MAIN CHANGES SINCE 1982

The single personal allowance has been raised to £1,785 from April 1983; the married allowance is £1,010 more than the single allowance.

The employee's national insurance contribution rate has been raised to 9 per cent, payable on the first £235 of gross weekly earnings by all employees earning £32,50 a week or more.

UNITED STATES(1)

1. INCOME TAX

a) Tax Unit

The members of a family may opt to be taxed in one of three ways:

- As a married couple filing jointly on the combined income of both spouses;
- As married individuals filing separately and reporting actual income of each spouse;
- As heads of households (only unmarried or separated individuals with dependants).

Dependent children with sufficient income file as single individuals.

b) Tax Allowances and Tax Credits

Basic: Since 1977, taxpayers are given a flat deduction amount called the "zero bracket amount" which is incorporated into each of the tax rate schedules as the lowest tax bracket carrying a zero tax rate. In 1982, the amounts, $2,300 for single individuals and $3,400 for married couples filing jointly. Taxpayers who elect to itemise were deducted only expenses in excess of the applicable zero bracket amount. In the case of separate returns of married persons, each spouse is entitled to a $1,700 zero bracket amount. However, if one spouse elects to itemise deductible expenses, the other spouse must do likewise. In this case, itemised deductions for one of the spouses may be less than the zero bracket amount, and the unused portion of the zero bracket amount must be added back to gross income in order to use the appropriate tax table or rate schedule. In addition to the above-mentioned deductions, a personal exemption of $1,000 is allowed for taxpayers and each dependant. State taxes are allowed as itemised deductions in computing federal taxes.

Marriage: No special deduction is provided for marriage, except joint returns are generally subject to preferential tax rates.

Children: A $1,000 exemption is given for dependants provided that over one half of the support is furnished by the taxpayer. Low-income workers with dependants are allowed a refundable credit equal to 10 per cent of earned income up to $5,000. If income exceeds $5,000 the credit is $500 less 12.5 per cent of the excess of income over $6,000.

c) Schedule

A different rate schedule is applicable to each of the three types of tax units described above. A fourth schedule is used by single persons.

---

1. In 1982 an Average Production Worker earned US$17,136.

The tax rates above the zero bracket amount range in each schedule from 12 to 50 per cent. The income levels at which each marginal rate is reached, however, differs considerably according to the different schedules.

d) Local Income Taxes

State and local taxes vary widely. In the examples chosen, the data refer to local taxes in Detroit, Michigan.

2. SOCIAL SECURITY CONTRIBUTIONS

a) Rate and Ceiling

The rate of contributions is 6.70 per cent of earnings up to $32,400 in 1982. This covers old age, disability, and death and hospitalisation. Employers also pay the same rate of tax on behalf of employees.

b) Distinction by Marital Status or Sex

None.

3. CASH TRANSFERS

a) Amount for Marriage

None.

b) Amount for Children

No general cash transfers exist, although low-income mothers qualifying for categorical welfare grants may receive cash transfers.

4. EFFECT ON TAX AND CASH TRANSFERS WHEN THE WIFE WORKS

a) On Husband's Allowances and Transfers

A two-earner married couple filing a joint return is allowed a deduction equal to 5 per cent of the earned income of the spouse with the lower amount of earnings. The deduction may not exceed $1,500.

b) Special Treatment for Wife

A child care allowance is granted under certain circumstances.

5. PRINCIPAL CHANGES SINCE 1982

a) An across-the-board tax rate cut of 8.75 per cent became effective.

b) The top rate on unearned income was lowered to 50 per cent from 70 per cent.

c) The deduction for two-earner married couples became effective.

d) The Social Security tax rate rose from 6.65 per cent to 6.7 per cent on maximum income of $32,400, up from $29,700.

V. SOURCES OF DATA/SOURCES DES DONNEES

SOURCE DES DONNEES UTILISEES POUR LE CALCUL DU REVENUE MOYEN D'UN OUVRIER

Allemagne	"Statistical Yearbook of Germany"
Australie	"Earnings and Hours of Employees", November, 1982, Australian Bureau of Statistics
Autriche	"Lohnstufenstatistik" et "Lohnnebenkostenstatistik"
Belgique	Office National de Securité Sociale, Rapport annuel 1982
Canada	Statistics Canada, Employment Earnings and Hours publications
Denmark	Danish Employers' Confederation
Etats-Unis	United States Department of Labor, Bureau of Labor Statistics
Finlande	Publication de l'Office Statistique "Wage Statistics"
France	"Comptes de la Nation"
Grèce	Service National de Statistiques de la Grèce et Organisme de Sécurité Sociale
Irlande	Bureau Central de Statistiques
Italie	Ministère du Travail Statistiques de l'emploi
Japon	Ministère de la Main-d'Oeuvre
Luxembourg	STATEC, Organismes de Sécurité Sociale, Ministère du Travail
Norvège	Norvègian Employers' Confederation
Nouvelle-Zélande	Quarterly Employment Survey by the Department of Labour
Pays-Bas	Central Bureau of Statistics
Portugal	Institut National de Statistique
Royaume-Uni	Department of Employment "New Earnings Survey"
Suède	Bureau National des Statiques
Suisse	Statistiques de l'Office fédéral de l'Industrie, des arts et métiers et du travail